ORGANIZATIONS IN THE MOVIES

The Legend of the Dysfunctional System

Stephen B. Sloane

University Press of America,® Inc.
Lanham · New York · Oxford

Copyright © 2002 by
University Press of America,® Inc.
4720 Boston Way
Lanham, Maryland 20706
UPA Acquisitions Department (301) 459-3366

PO Box 317
Oxford
OX2 9RU, UK

All rights reserved
Printed in the United States of America
British Library Cataloging in Publication Information Available

Library of Congress Cataloging-in-Publication Data

Sloane, Stephen B.
Organizations in the movies : the legend of the
dysfunctional system / Stephen B. Sloane.
p. cm
Includes bibliographical references and index.
1. Organizational behavior in motion pictures. I. Title.

PN1995.9.O75 S59 2002
791.43'655—dc21   2002035997 CIP

ISBN 0-7618-2434-0 (paperback : alk. ppr.)

∞™ The paper used in this publication meets the minimum
requirements of American National Standard for Information
Sciences—Permanence of Paper for Printed Library Materials,
ANSI Z39.48—1984

For Kit

Who has taught me that imagination is more
important than knowledge
and
That persistence is more important than either

Contents

Preface		vii
Acknowledgements		xi
Chapter 1	Seeking the Truth in Fiction	1
Chapter 2	The Silver Screen and the Organizational Setting	11
Chapter 3	Fragility of Harmony The case of *Network*	23
Chapter 4	Complexity of Purpose The case of *Twelve O'clock High*	37
Chapter 5	The Problem of Multiple Roles The cases of: *Electric Horseman; In Pursuit of Honor; Lost in America*	49
Chapter 6	The Problem of Isolation The case of *Groundhog Day*	59
Chapter 7	The Problem of Location: Hierarchy The cases of: *Twelve O'clock High; Patton; The Caine Mutiny; Catch 22*	71
Chapter 8	The Problem of Location: Specialization The case of *Executive Suite*	83
Chapter 9	The Problem of Professionalism The cases of: *The Right Stuff; A Few Good Men*	91

Chapter 10 Fear of the Future	105
The cases of: *2001 A Space Odyssey; Rollerball*	
Chapter 11 Coping Strategies; Directing Your Own Movie	115
Chapter 12 Conclusion	133
References	136
Index	138

Preface

When I became a member of the faculty at a liberal arts college, my formal training in the liberal arts was nil. I had earned degrees in engineering, public administration and political science. All of these were based on thoroughly modern paradigms, on the idea that nature, the way the world works, is best explained by using methods of objective observation and analysis. This generated the *text* that justified my qualification to enter academia.

The *context* of my capability to teach and to study, my life experience, had caused me, however, to question the usefulness of thought that eschewed imagination. Descartes, I knew, had demonstrated to himself and others that reasoned thought generated the proof of human existence. It followed from this that truth finding should rely exclusively on man's ability to reason.

The more I was jostled by the ebb and flow of my own experience, the more I came into contact with the human condition, the more convinced I became that my own existence was confirmed by imagination and not by objective logic. For Descartes and his followers, the mantra was, "I think therefore I am." Much more attractive to me, however, was the notion that the reality of my existence took the form of the image that I held of myself. Logic might be expressed in words and numbers. Image, however, was expressed in pictures. And since one picture might capture the essence of thousands of words or numbers, the complexity of my own humanity and the richness of human experience, it seemed to me, would be more truly captured by images.

Moreover, I was put off by the notion that the very process of objective analysis implies that there is one big Answer. This suggests a sense of inevitability. If The Question has already been answered, or is soon to be answered, then I am not in control of my own fate. On the other hand, if I have the power of imagination, the power to create the pictures that form the reality of my own existence, I am in control. I discovered that an anti-Cartesian attitude was liberating.

As a very junior professor, liberation from the precepts of mainstream science, social or otherwise, would by a pyrrhic victory. So I kept my thoughts to myself. The assignment to teach courses in my college's great books seminar program, however, started my liberal education and my liberation from the restrictive aspects of previous formal education. The great books represented man's most noble attempts to find answers to important questions. All these books may have been great, but all did not espouse the same truth. More important, these celebrated works of truth searching often took the form of stories. Some great books were not even books. They were pictures of Grecian urns, depictions of one image of Athena or another! Stories and pictures as truth finders... how nice.

I had studied war as a social scientist. I had experienced war. Homer told me more about the consequences of war than even the best analysis provided by books and mentors or by my own reflections on personal experience. I had studied capitalism and experienced life as *economic man*. Dickens' images revealed much more truth concerning the meaning of economics and the consequences of capitalism. I had examined and experienced the political environment of the civil rights movement. Toni Morrison provided me with images that were considerably more informative concerning matters of race in America. I had reflected on the values of feminism and on the causes and consequences of the push of women toward gender equity. Such reflection produced limited understanding compared to the images evoked by Sapho and by Virginia Wolfe. The great books that form the nucleus of liberal education, I discovered, provided the mortar that held together the bricks of objective reasoning. This was the mortar of *meaning*. Once the facts were gathered, once cause and effect relationships were established, the question, "So what?" still had to be dealt with.

Such liberation might free one to turn his focus in any direction. My focus, for reasons that will be explained as the reader works his way through the following chapters, turned toward man as a member of modern organizations. The fresh air provided by such liberation encouraged me to deal with the concept of human happiness, as proposed by Aristotle, in the context of man's experience as a participant in the activities of modern organizations.

The images to draw upon in a liberated search for enlightenment concerning the relationship between people and their organizations can come from many sources. The sources that I have used here are the stories that artists, screenwriters, actors and directors tell through the media of film. These stories describe and explain conflict between organized systems and the human parts that comprise these systems. There are many films that I might have used in an endeavor to answer the question, "So what?" These chapters reveal my favorites...so far.

Acknowledgment

When I entered the Naval Academy nearly fifty years ago, I was assigned to a summer company for the purpose of undergoing Plebe indoctrination. It was a long hot summer, filled with little by way of academics and much by way of athletics and professional training (read that as marching with a heavy rifle and shining shoes to a mirror-like gloss).

I was given the opportunity to volunteer for one form or another of athletic activity. Here I would compete with other summer companies of Plebes and learn an important lesson for future navy professionals, the importance of winning. As a city boy who had played basketball, football, and baseball in high school, I was fascinated with the thought of rowing on a team of eight that propelled sleek fragile wooden boats, shells, down the Severn River in exhausting races pitted against other crews. I volunteered for the sport of crew.

The leader of my company was a newly graduated Ensign, assigned to stay on for the summer to manage the initial socialization of we future naval officers. I do not remember his name.

Our Ensign's own dedication to winning was an example for us all. He had one problem, at least one that I know of. His important company boxing team lacked a heavyweight. My own weight was plenty heavy and I had boxed as a youngster in summer camp. The Ensign informed me that I should forget the sport of crew and sign on as the heavyweight member of the company boxing team. I assumed that the word *volunteer,* as it applied to choosing a sport, was meant literally. I assumed that I had the discretion to pick and choose the venue for the spilling of my sweat in the cause of   company glory. In some respects I was right. In some respects I was wrong. I informed my Ensign that I was *volunteering* for crew. He did not seem happy about this. I did not think his unhappiness was relevant to my situation.

As part of our marching activity we would undergo daily rifle inspection. Each day we spent many hours disassembling and cleaning our nearly antique M-1 rifles. Mine was spotless, inside and out. So were the rifles of all my peers. I believed that the teaching point here was that if we expected a weapon to take care of us in combat, we needed to take care of the weapon. That turned out *not* to be the teaching point.

On the day following my insistence on volunteering for the crew team, as we stood at "inspection arms" our Ensign walked down the ranks, rapidly snatching the rifle from the hands of each Midshipman, quickly glancing at the external condition of the weapon, holding the barrel to his eye allowing daylight to flow from the muzzle to the chamber, searching for any spot of dirt. As he held up my rifle in this manner, he exclaimed, "This is filthy!" I was aghast and he could see that I was. "Here," he said, "Look for   yourself." I looked. I saw the lining of the barrel and it shone with pristine brilliance. "It's clean, sir," I proclaimed. "It is filthy," he responded, the sparkling brand new gold bars highlighting the starched collar of his khaki uniform And he followed this with the assignment of an appropriate number of demerits and, more important, with punishment consisting of a considerable number of hours of marching off extra duty in my practically nonexistent spare time.

It is from this Officer that I learned the *Golden Rule of Leadership and Management*: "He who has the gold, makes the rule!"

It is here that I thank the Ensign for a long delayed subliminal inspiration to write this book.

Chapter One

Seeking the Truth in Fiction

> "Remember, the point of life is to be happy. All other goals (money, fame, status, responsibility, achievement) are merely ways of making you happy. They are worthless in themselves."
> *True Professionalism,* David H. Maister

This book is a response to Robert Pirsig's advice, in *Zen And The Art Of Motorcycle Maintenance,* to explore "... that strange separation of what man is from what man does (to find) some clues as to what the hell has gone wrong in this twentieth century." (Persig 1974) It seems to me, as we enter the twenty first century, that the tension between what it means to be a human *doer* and what it means to be a human *being* is most evident when we consider the role of man as a participant in the activities of organizations.

In the following pages I want to make these arguments:
- Organizational systems are a potential, if not common, source of unhappiness for organizational members.
- The stories told by movies are a form of *administrative fiction* that can help us explain and understand conflict between organizations and their members.
- This understanding can encourage the development of effective survival skills and coping mechanisms.

Since my method of investigation involves the telling of stories, perhaps I should start with: Once upon a time...

When I sat down to lunch with three friends I had not seen for some time, I expected the conversation to be technical and professional. It was our working lives that had brought us together in the past. Now we were meeting as old friends, a sort of reunion. All of us are experienced professionals: two professors and two retired naval officers. Our common working interest and expertise is the study of modern organizations in general and specifically the vulnerability of some organizations to serious, costly, irreversible errors (plane crashes, collisions at sea, nuclear meltdowns, etc.).

As longtime practitioners, as well as students, of the art of organizational life, we had plenty of *data* to chew over. Our experience was theoretical and bookish as well as empirical and real world. We did not have to ask superficial questions to start a conversation, questions like "Have you seen any good movies lately?" Yet the first words uttered were, "Have you seen the movie *Titanic*?" From there the conversation turned to the proposition that if the ship had not been turned in a vain attempt to avoid the iceberg, she would have hit it straight on and would not have been fatally damaged. Then we went on to discuss other movies that vibrated sympathetically with our interest in error and disaster: *China Syndrome... Doctor Strangelove... Towering Inferno...*

It seemed odd that we who considered ourselves to be practitioners of social science as well as thoroughly modern, if not scientific, managers and leaders, wanted to focus our attention on fiction, the movies; but maybe this was not so very odd. Fiction, after all, can be a powerful source of truth, the sort of truth that cannot be revealed by mere facts, the sort of truth that divulges the *meaning* of what we experience and observe, what we are, what it takes to make us happy, or miserable, the sort of truth that can lead us from an examination of the *trees* to an understanding of the *forest* or perhaps, more appropriate to the issue of organizational life, the *jungle*.

Later, when I thought about the lunch and the conversation that centered on disaster movies, I thought that we had avoided discussing what might be the most persistent disaster of all: the day to day internal battles that go on between organizations and the individuals that are the parts that make up the whole organized system, organizational members. I thought about the stresses of organizational life.

The tension between individual and communal needs is one problem that has always been part of civilized human experience. The individual needs the group and the group needs the individual. Yet the group can get in the way of individuality. Membership in an organizational community that becomes an obstacle to happiness is a specific case of this universal human predicament.

Aristotle suggested that happiness is:

> What is always chosen as an end in itself and never as a means to somethingelse [but rather] is called final in an unqualified sense. This description seems to apply to happiness above all else: for we always choose happiness as an end in itself and never for the sake of something else. (Aristotle 1962,15)

If we accept Aristotle's definition, and the stories discussed here implicitly do, it becomes apparent that it may be reasonable to expect the rewards, material and otherwise, that are provided by our organization.

But these rewards are only the *means* to valued ends. And, as the stories examined in the following chapters will reveal, costs can be incurred when one participates in organizational activities that exceed the benefits. Moreover, we cannot rely on our membership or our cooperation in the processes of the organization as a *direct source* of happiness. The organization simply cannot be relied upon to *make* us happy because the organization is not, in Aristotle's words, "... an end in itself." This is evident because whatever the "ends" are for the organization, these are not *necessarily* the same as the "ends" sought by the individual, or the ends that will satisfy the needs of the individual.

Why should we look to the silver screen for help in explaining and understanding the conflict between organizations and their members? How can the stories told by movies suggest ways of dealing with this problem, ways to develop survival skills and coping mechanisms? Are there recurring themes that illuminate the way that organizational man falls into the trap of failing to distinguish his *being* from his *doing*?

Stories are a rich source of wisdom. Stories, in particular those that are told and retold, can artfully reveal significant truths concerning the human condition. Art not only imitates life, it also makes an attempt to understand, to explain life, to lead us to a deeper comprehension of what it means to be a human being. A story becomes a legend if its substance is revealed over and over again in many different contexts or circumstances. Native American stories of creation are told by describing situations that are very different than those of Judeo-Christian stories of creation. Greek stories of heroism and tragedy take a different form from those of Scandinavian cultures. Stories do tell us about the differences of time and place. Yet stories of creation, or tragedy, or heroism, can tell us even more about the common anatomy of humanity than they can about the differing circumstances of various human cultures or communities. The enduring stories of all cultures have many things in common even though the cultures are not at all connected. There are stories of creation, of flood and destruction, of redemption, of heroism and villainy, in all cultures. Even though the form of the story may vary, the substance of the story does not vary and neither does the substantive truth revealed by the tale. These stories advance to the status of myth or legend.

What sort of picture do the stories told in moves paint concerning the ecstasy and the agony of organizational life? Movies about organizations and the people who participate in the activities of organizations show us a picture that is not "pretty". In *Twelve O'clock High*, the 918th Bomber Group fails to put its bombs on target, is plagued by high losses of flying crews, and is threatened to be put out of existence by German fighters and flack. In *Network*, the United Broadcasting System is in danger of being swallowed up by a giant conglomerate. The organization is losing the battle of the ratings as well as the commitment of the members of its News Department. *The Firm* shows us an organization that captures its members by taking advantage of their lust for material gain, luxury and conspicuous consumption. *Devil's Advocate* paints the same picture, in perhaps a more dramatic way. The police department of *Serpico* is corrupt. The main characters in *Lost in America, Jerry McGuire* and *Electric Cowboy* flee from their corporations to search for happiness. Movies like these are the stuff of the Legend Of The Dysfunctional System, the legend of the organization that may be working just fine, given the ends that it pursues, and not working at all, given the ends that satisfy the human needs of its members. How does the Legend lead us to a deeper understanding?

Most of what we have discovered, most of what we *know* about organizations comes to us by way of the efforts of social scientists, by way of the domains of social psychology and administrative science. There is an enormous body of theory that attempts to explain, and indeed does explain, what is observed in the environment of organizations. From this theoretical understanding, and within the domains of public and business administration, management and leadership principles are derived. Theory and the practice of organizations is studied and learned in the academic environment that supports the practice of management. All of this is subsumed by the rubric of *administration*. Because of the very nature of its boundaries, the formal study of administration is conducted (predominately) from a social system perspective, one that focuses on the behavior and purpose of the organized system, rather than on the individual perspective. Those who study the behavior of individuals are involved in the realm of psychology rather than administration. They are dealing with the parts of the system rather than the whole. For the administrative scientist, since he is interested in the nature of the whole, reducing the focus of study exclusively to the individual can lead to error. Such a reduction in the unit of analysis, for example, might lead us to try to understand the nature or the effectiveness of a baseball team by way of knowledge of the batting averages of each team member. The batting average of a player tells us about the player (as a unit of analysis) but not about the team as a system that is designed and managed for the purpose of winning games.

When the administrative scientist or professional does use the ideas of the psychologist, he does so more to understand or influence organizational outcomes than to appreciate the human consequences of organizational activity. The work of the psychologist Abraham Maslow, for example, demonstrated that human needs can best be understood in terms of a hierarchy ranging from survival, to associational, to esteem, to self-actualization. (Maslow,1954) In that self-actualization is at the highest end of this ladder of human needs, Maslow comes close to capturing Aristotle's conception of happiness in psychological rather than philosophical terms. Maslow tells us that the lower level needs have to be satisfied before the higher level needs become operative. Maslow's ideas, however, are not studied by emerging managers in order to understand the process of achieving human actualization (happiness). They are rather studied for the purpose of developing more effective motivational strategies that will enable managers to control employee behavior by controlling the expectation of reward (need fulfillment).

We should not be surprised that the prescriptions for the practice of management that are derived from formal (scientific) knowledge most often look through the lens of the organization. We should not be surprised that so much energy at schools of public and business administration focuses on the subjects of leadership, policy, strategy and decision making and so little on philosophy and the humanities. Plato's *Republic* specified the ideal leader as a "philosopher king." This is an attempt to synthesize what man is with what man does. But that is a concept that is way outside the modern study of administration. The leader-manager and not the philosopher king designs and operates the organizational system. Leader-managers are responsible for organizational outcomes. The leader-manager accepts the formal mission of the organization and the health of the organization as the core of his ethics. A leader whose ethical profile caused him consistently to resolve conflict between the needs of individuals and organizations in favor of individuals would no longer be a leader. That is what happens to Colonel Keith Davenport in *Twelve O'clock High*. That is what happens to the compassionate but confused Executive Officer Steve Maryk in *The Caine Mutiny*.

The problem examined *here* is the problem of conflict within organizations as viewed from the perspective of the *individual*. Schools of public and business administration do not really study or teach the subject of *individual* happiness in the context of the organizational setting. If they did they would no longer be schools of administration (qua administration). The dominant paradigm in the field of *Administration* excludes a philosophy of happiness. The injection of art into the study of administration would modify this paradigm.

The point has been made that the social scientist and the administrative *engineers* that put the principles discovered by the social scientist to use see organizational life predominately through the lens of the organized system. Does the artist have a different perspective? If so, what is the perspective of the artist? How can art contribute to understanding?

Dwight Waldo has contributed a great deal of wisdom to the study of administration. He also appreciates fiction. He tells us that the social scientist and the artist (writer of stories) function in two different worlds. Each has something to give that the other cannot. In the modern world, we are all aware of what the scientist contributes to progress. Yet a more complete understanding of the complex ways the human condition and administrative structures mix, claims Waldo, requires the insight and the imagination that is brought to us by the teller of stories. (Waldo 1968)

Waldo suggests that the administrative scientist and the teller of stories each has a distinct contribution to make. The former can tell us about the situation and problems of the system. The latter, since he looks at life from the bias of the individual and examines life at a level of analysis of the individual, can tell us more about the situation and the problems of the human participant.

If you want to improve the performance of a baseball team (evidenced as games won) go to an expert manager. We do that when we study, in a formal way, the science of administration and its applications.

If you want to improve the performance your batting average (the purpose of serving your own individual interests) go to a batting coach. Perhaps that is what we can do when we study administrative fiction. If you are only interested in the fulfilling the mission of the team and you see no possibility of a conflict between your interest and that of the team, if you want to be an *organization-person,* then learn how to get hit with the pitched ball without the umpire discerning that you did so on purpose. (In baseball jargon that is called "... taking one for the team!") That is what we do when we fail to study or reflect upon our organizational lives in a careful and imaginative way.

Waldo also tells us that there is a fine line between our accumulation of experience, the nonfiction component of our *story*, and the way that we project the images of our imaginative perception onto this *story*, the fictional component (Waldo 1968, 25). He tells us that "an imaginative construction may flow from much personal experience, and a good one almost of necessity does; a reconstruction from memory will inevitably have a fictional component."

The study of fictional cases is a useful complement to experience. Waldo also points out (Waldo 1968) that the study of fiction can reveal a much more elegant and complete portrayal of the organizational landscape. Here we have an opportunity to observe, under widely differing conditions and in varying perspectives, a "whole" situation, one in which politics (or policy) and administration are joined by an act of artistic synthesis rather than separated by an act of scientific analysis.

He goes on to tell us that science experiments by controlling variables, an all other things are equal methodology. But in the fictional story, all other things are not equal. The story can thereby capture the full complexity of circumstance in a way that is not available to the scientific method.

Whereas Waldo emphasizes the separate perspectives of science and art, Charles Goodsell and Nancy Murray suggest that useful conceptual bridges can be constructed to span the perceived gulfs that separate the rational and scientific study of administration and the arts. The analysis of film stories that follows builds some of these bridges. (Goodsell and Murray 1995)

First of all, is the bridge that connects theory and the arts. Aesthetic inquiry considers the individual's place in an overarching view of beauty (and by implication ugliness). The film stories discussed here all focus on the relationship of the individual to his circumstance and environment. This can lead to a deeper theoretical understanding of the organizational system.

A second bridge pertains to values. Film stories bring us insights not normally attainable in the classroom or on the job. The stories translate into concrete form those concepts that are norm-laden such as power, ambition, survival and vision.

Careful examination and analysis encourages us to examine our own values and to evaluate our own situations in ways that we would not otherwise contemplate.

Goodsell and Murray's teaching bridge is perhaps most relevant to the analyses presented in this book. They tell us that "Enthusiasts of administrative fiction have argued for some years that one of the few ways we have to transmit the subtleties of administrative processes to novice students [and I would add to seasoned practitioners] in an otherwise sterile classroom is through novels or film." (Goodselll and Murray 1995) Examination of fiction results in vicarious experience and can help develop intuitive survival skills.

Moreover, consideration of film stories as cases can illuminate important and powerful abstractions, can make them accessible and relevant to the lives of the viewer.

Chapter Two

The Silver Screen and the Organizational Setting

"For it is for the sake of the end that all else is done."
Nicomachean Ethics, Aristotle

Movie scenarios illuminate the happiness definition of the great Greek philosopher as it applies to organizational life. Mr. Happer, the Chief Executive Officer of Knox Oil, in *Local Hero,* seems to be the personification of the organization. If anyone is going to accept an organization as an end in itself, it will be the person at the top. After all, if the organization succeeds, he succeeds. Yet, Happer is wise enough (in the view of his therapist, crazy enough) to realize that even the CEO cannot depend on the organization as a source of happiness. Accordingly, Happer uses Knox Oil and the rewards he gleans from his position at Knox Oil to pursue his serious interest in astronomy. For Happer, Knox Oil is an instrumental value and astronomy is a terminal value.

Sometimes the individual terminal values that need to be satisfied are not apparent, even to a leader. In *Twelve O'clock High*, the Commanding Officer, General Savage, acts as though the bombing success of the 918th Bomber Group is, for him, a terminal value, an end in and of itself. If the 918th succeeds, he will be happy. At least it seems so to Savage.

But the story tells us, by way of Savage's unhappy nervous breakdown, that the value of the lives of his men became of paramount importance. The story tells us that the preservation of these lives was a human value that Savage could not put aside, a terminal value that he could not ignore in his role as a leader.

A fundamental condition of organizational life is that the interests of the organization as a whole and those of the members of the organization are not inherently the same. When discussing international relations, Henry Kissinger was quick to point out that among nations there are neither permanent friends nor permanent enemies, only permanent interests. The stories described by movies tell us that the same is true with respect to the relations between organizations and their members. The organization and its members *may* be friends in those conditions where conflict between them does not exist. But this *friendship* is not *permanent*.

Failure to recognize the lack of inherent, predictable, permanent, harmony between the organized system and its members can lead to disillusionment. Organizational participants are vulnerable to disappointment and frustration because organizational leaders attempt, and more often than not succeed at, socializing members. Organizational life, from the *cradle* to the *grave* involves the experience of being encouraged, if not seduced, to accept the values of the organization, to merge the ends sought by the individual with those sought by the organization, to accept the values *specified* by the organization. Those rewards that an individual receives as a result of participation depend on the acceptance of socialization. The most intensely socialized members are the most generously rewarded. Savage in *Twelve O'clock High* is, at least in part, a General because he has accepted the values, indeed the culture, of the Army Air Corps as his own.

The process of socialization enables participants successfully to adapt to the organizational environment. At the same time, as many of the stories examined here suggest, socialization can be a not so tender trap. For Lieutenant Bishop in *Twelve O'clock High* and for Howard in *Network,* the consequence of socialization is death. And to make things worse, the invidious consequences of socialization are not always apparent. One reason for this is that the stability and effectiveness of an organization depends, at times, on the ability of leaders to disguise the potential injurious impact of socialization. General Savage asks his men to consider themselves to be already dead.In effect, he is saying, "Do not worry about dying as a consequence of your socialization." In the movie *Silkwood* the managers of Kerr-McGee tell their employees that radiation at the plant is within acceptable limits.This is a blatant attempt to hide the cost of socialization...cancer. The essence of leadership strategy is to find ways of dealing with latent strain between what it takes to make the individual happy and what it takes to make the organization happy. The literature of organization theory, the suggestions of management consulting gurus, and movie stories are saturated with this notion.

It has been noted (Etzioni 1964) that there is a wide range of types of organizations that vary according to the way that participants are encouraged to conform to organizational requirements. These include normative pressure (such as we find in religious and front line military organizations), utilitarian inducement (the generic corporation), and the use of force (prisons).

All of these types are illuminated by movie stories.In *High Noon* the sheriff risks his life to save the town because he believes that is the right thing to do. He tries to convince his deputies to join him by using moral persuasion. Here the organization is *normative*. Most of the employees in the movie *Silkwood* risk exposure to nuclear radiation because they need the job. The organization is utilitarian. And in a host of prison movies from *White Heat*, to *The Birdman of Alcatraz* to *The Shawshank Redemption*, members of a prison organization (convicts) are induced to cooperate by the use or the threat of force. Regardless of where the organization fits into Etzioni's typology of organizations, the leader attempts to induce the follower to accept the needs of the organized system.

One management guru (Morgan 1997) more recently

encourages leaders to suggest various images of the organization that followers should consider. One of the most powerful of these is the image of the holograph. The relevance of the analogy of the holograph is that each of the parts of the holographic image contains all of the elements of the whole. The implication is that each participant, once the image is accepted as a normative model, will be a miniature of the whole organization. The movie *The Spy Who Shagged Me* comes to mind. Here the villain, Dr. Evil, creates a miniature clone of himself, Mini-Me. And Mini-Me fulfills the aspirations of Dr. Evil as nobody else can.

According to Morgan, leaders need to "find ways of organizing through shared visions, values, and cultures." (Morgan 1997,176). In terms of the holographic analogy, "shared," means the total transformation of the parts (individuals) so as to replicate in miniature the whole (organization), i.e. to become Mini-Mes, to become socialized. The movie *1984* is an even more thoughtful examination of an attempt to socialize thoroughly.

Chester I. Barnard, in his classic revelation of *The Functions of the Executive* (Barnard 1938) developed a notion of efficiency based on the concept of individual *zone of indifference*. Barnard proposed that the idea of efficiency previously adhered to by leaders, the idea of optimal output for a given resource utilization, was not useful. He proposed, rather, that efficiency was achieved by way of the mobilization of human resources. And this could best be achieved, according to Barnard, by limiting the requirements that organizations placed on participants to a *zone of indifference*. This means issuing "...orders (that) are acceptable (to the individual) without conscious questioning of... authority" (Barnard 1938, 167). Orders that are within one's *zone of indifference* are accepted without the necessity to provide additional incentives that would draw on the organization's resources (material or otherwise).

In the movie *Local Hero*, the title character accepts orders to effect a land purchase in Scotland. He accepts the orders without reservation, even though the environmental and social impact of the purchase is questionable. By implication, the acceptability of an order without the conscious questioning of authority or legitimacy, depends on the extent of socialization. The order is accepted indifferently because the *local hero* is well socialized, at least at the start of the film story.

If I accepted Morgan's image of the holograph, I would consider myself to be the personification of the organization. My aspirations and those of the organization would coincide. My *zone of indifference* would be very wide and I would accept orders without the necessity of any incentive other than my continuing membership. This was the case with most of the Kerr-McGee employees in *Silkwood*. Karen Silkwood, to the contrary, vehemently resisted the company's attempt at encouraging her to accept a radiation hazard. Her zone of indifference was very narrow and the consequential inefficiency of the corporation's attempt to gain control of her is demonstrated by the eventual demise of both Karen *and* the plant that employed her. In many of the stories that we shall examine, the dangers of socialization for the individual are dramatically revealed.

The pressure for the organization to gain some level of control of the individual results in the persistence of bureaucracy as an organizing principle. In that the organization is hierarchical, the decision process tends to be centralized and orders flow from top to bottom. In that rules are designed to effect predictability and efficiency, individual discretion is limited. In that labor is divided into specialized pockets of activity, the range of individual activity is restricted. (Weber 1946)

A good deal of theoretical and practical literature that deals with the management of organizations either proposes that the bureaucratic form is going out of fashion or prescribes alternative leadership styles and organization designs. The intention is either to prescribe or to describe a transformation from the bureaucratic machine to a design more appropriate to the dynamics of the postmodern world. Yet the bureaucratic structure is neither dead nor dying.

Those who consider the way the individual self (or soul, if you will) can be damaged by an organization often suggest or demonstrate structural change that might cure or mitigate organizational and human pathologies that can be traced to the dominance of the bureaucratic form. But these thinkers most often fail to account for the persistence of the bureaucratic form. Yes, it would be nice if the organization development gurus who desire managers to encourage self-organization and the use of images and imagination to deal with the fast moving pace of the chaotic and globalized business and political world all ruled organizations. But they do not.Perhaps the popularity of the organization development genre as well as the desire to reinvent government are indications that there is a lot of pain out there and much striving to mitigate the pain.

Morgan's use of the holograph metaphor (Morgan 1997) has already been mentioned. Morgan also tells us how the image of a spider plant can be used as an evocative springboard for thinking about organizing in a decentralized manner. He suggests other images such as octopi, amoebas, spiders, supernovas and dandelions seeds, that can be used to " create a shared appreciation of the ideas and principles on which an organization builds and the role (that can be played) in helping maintain unconventional (i.e. non-bureaucratic) forms." (Morgan 1997,125) The results of such imagining, he says, can be the total integration of the units (i.e. humans) into the process of the whole system (i.e. organization). These are proposed cures for the bureaucratic disease.

Another author tells us that in nature, rational cooperation can be achieved in the absence of the bureaucratic form of organizing. *The Heart Aroused* (Whyte, 1996) suggests an image that might help organizations deal with the complex, even chaotic, organizational environment of today and the future. Chaos theory, tells us that a flock of Starlings maintains the orderly shape of its formation as each bird conforms to a few simple rules, such as maintaining a minimum distance from other objects. The flock is a "bottom up" adaptive decision structure unlike the "top down" machine-like bureaucracy. In this way the survival requirement of each bird (less vulnerability to flying predators like hawks) is fulfilled without the necessity for a strategic design that is prescribed by a boss bird. And the requirement of the system (species) to survive is also enhanced.

But if we look more closely at the image of the flock of Starlings we can see that this is a natural, as compared to a man made, system. Nature programs each bird, indeed hard wires each bird, with the few simple rules that can create order and harmony out of complexity and chaos. Humans are not at all programmed with a few simple rules that can bring order and coordination out of complexity and chaos. If we were, then the dominate method of design would indeed be that of self-organizing instead of bureaucracy. We humans have to learn the rules that might turn chaos into order. The flock of Starlings is not at all self-organizing. Starlings do not design the organization of the flock. They simply do not have the free will to do that. Nature designs the organization of the flock. Man, who is both blessed and cursed with free will, designs his own organized systems. Whereas nature prescribes rules that are functional for birds in the flock, man does not come with a hard wired program consisting of such a functional design. So the boss man or woman takes on this responsibility, at least most of the time. It may not be fair to ask people to be as adaptive as birds. Thus, bureaucracy persists as a fact of organizational life. And what is functional for the bureaucratic organizational system is neither naturally nor by design functional for the human beings that are the parts of the system.

Of course, organizations at times do behave in adaptive ways, we might even say natural or organic ways that transcend machine-like bureaucracy. Karl Weick describes the self-organizing capacity of NASA as this organization devolves decision making authority to orbiting astronauts (Weick 1990). Weick and Karlene Roberts tell us how the flight deck crews on aircraft carriers cope with complexity by responding to seemingly chaotic situations in adaptive ways that cannot be expained in terms of orders, rules, regulations. (Weick and Roberts, 1993)

The seminal work on the difference between computer and human intelligence, *Man Over Machine*, makes the observation that that experts, who can occupy positions at the lower levels of a hierarchy, make efficacious decisions based on intuition rather than by following rule based formulae that are the heart and soul of bureaucracy. (Dreyfus and Dreyfus 1986)

Yet these observations do not demonstrate that bureaucracy is no longer a useful form of organizing. Neither do they describe nor predict the demise of bureaucracy. What they do signify is that in conditions where the centralized control mechanisms of bureaucracy are insufficient to cope with the extent of complexity and uncertainty at hand, organizations (or more appropriately teams of people that are subsystems of the whole) can and do act more like adaptive organisms than machines. In such conditions, central authority can and often will devolve decision authority to lower level participants. But this process does not melt bureaucracy like water melted the Wicked Witch of the West in *The Wizard of Oz*.

When the flight deck crews described by Weick and Roberts complete flight operations, they come off the deck and return to a highly structured bureaucratic environment. Once the astronauts come down to earth they come down to a bureaucratic NASA. And here on earth it is less likely that those in a position of authority will recognize that the complexity and uncertainty of a given circumstance merits the devolution of authority to lower level participants (professionals). The *Challenger* disaster is a case in point. Those (engineers) who wanted to cancel the launch simply did not have the authority to do so. In the case of *Challenger*, the persistence of hierarchical decision-making in an inappropriate circumstance is clearly demonstrated.

The movie *Apollo 13* (the telling of a true story in a dramatic way) illustrates self-organizing design. Once it was decided that "Failure is not an option!" the authority of decision making was passed to experts who heretofore occupied positions at lower levels in the organization.

Of course, those who made the *Challenger* launch decision in the face of what appeared to be minor problems caused by cold weather did not consider failure to be an option. Yet the possibility of failure was not nearly as apparent as it was in the case of *Apollo 13* or as it is apparent in the case of (even routine) aircraft carrier operations. When bureaucracy is *clearly* a formula for disaster, bureaucracy tends to melt. But such clarity is the exception rather than the rule.

The struggle between the organizational whole, which acts like a machine, and the organizational participant's desire to act as a human adaptive organism is clearly illuminated in the battle for control between the astronaut Dave and the computer Hal in the movie *2001*. Hal's intelligence is artificial. Hal has been programmed by the organization. Dave's aspirations and fears are human.

Sometimes, lower level participants who recognize the necessity to escape from central control to achieve success will deceive their leaders into a devolution of authority. In this way employees can be loyal to the organization's mission by being disloyal to their employers. In *Twelve O'clock High*, General Savage believes it is necessary to continue the flight of the 918th Bomber Group toward its target even though his boss, General Pritchard, recalls the aircraft due to bad weather. Savage decouples his aircraft formations from Pritchard's headquarters by faking radio failure. He thereby releases himself from the duty of returning to home base, from the duty to follow orders. Once he gets back to base, however, Savage finds himself quite tightly coupled to the bureaucratic chain of command. He is once again under the thumb of his boss. And although Pritchard clearly appreciates Savages heroism, he unequivocally admonishes Savage to "...avoid gambling with my chips."

Bureaucracy can be modified or even melted in certain conditions. But these are special circumstances that do not describe the experience of most people most of the time. Most people, most of the time are vulnerable to experiencing the sort of unhappiness that is of concern here.

Much has been written about leadership and on the function of leaders to mitigate the conflict between the organized system and its human parts. The Human Relations paradigm of theory, including the seminal work of Argyris (Argyris 1957) and the more practical ideas of Barnard come to mind. (Barnard 1938) Those who ran Harvard's Hawthorne Plant investigation for General Electric discovered that production increased even in worsening work conditions. Workers mistakenly perceived that the investigators' presence demonstrated employer interest and concern for their day-to-day circumstances. And the result was increased motivation and increased production. (Roethlisberger 1941) Leaders would henceforth be seen as capable of using their skills to meld the human and the structural components of organizations into well oiled harmoniously functioning systems.

The point has already been made that the capacity for self-organization to overcome the invidious impact of bureaucracy depends on the details of the situation. The capacity of leaders to mitigate conflict between human and organizational needs is also contingency dependent. In the movie *Lost In America*, David serves his advertising agency for 8 years and climbs the ladder of success to lead the creative development section of the firm. His boss has frequently shared lunch and painted a rosy picture of David's future with the firm. David is happy. David is productive. Leadership works just fine. Then the situation changes. The firm is given the lucrative Ford account and needs David to move from Los Angeles to New York to help develop the campaign. David, however, has aspirations to be promoted to Executive Vice President. Acting in what he perceives to be the best interest of the firm, the boss selects another person for the Vice President job and attempts to convince David to move to New York. One day the leader is doing just fine. On the next day his order is so far out of David's zone of indifference that David's pain sends him into a self-destructive rage.

One common contingency factor that incapacitates the leader's ability to orchestrate harmony is the condition of scarce resources. General Savage, for example, was prohibited from giving his aircrews a reasonable expectation of survival by releasing them after a finite number of missions because replacements were not available. In *Twelve O'clock High*, the contingency is that the men fly until they die. Savage is a pretty good leader but there is no way that he can have happiness and organizational effectiveness at the same time. In the heyday of the birth of the "dot com" revolution, leaders could make everybody happy because the resource (money) pie seemed to be infinitely large. But when the pie shrank the heyday was over and the rational option for leaders was to sacrifice people in an attempt to effect the survival of the organization.

In the movie *The Americanization of Emily* a Navy Admiral perceives that the D Day invasion of Europe will be a public relations triumph for the Army and its Air Corps. He decides that the solution to this problem is to be sure that the first man to die on Omaha beach is a sailor. And a fellow officer attempts to shoot the first man to die. Here, when a leader perceives that the organization is threatened (in this case by the U.S. Army) the leaders job is not to meld individual and organizational interest, but rather to sacrifice the individual.

Waldo makes the point that we cannot depend on leadership to always save the day, He tells us:

> Barnard, without in any sense being narrowly moralistic found the essence of the executive function and of responsibility to rest in what to him was an area of morality. Both as experienced executive and as student he was impressed with the tremendous moral complexity to be found in an organization, in the intersection of private and public, objective and subjective moral codes and sentiments. The severest test of the executive's skill and stamina, he found, is in his ability to deal creatively, as he saw it morally with moral complexity. If he does not have the skill and stamina, he will fail to perform adequately, competitively; if he is too weak for

his tasks he may well be destroyed, one way or another. It seems to me inevitable that the struggle to maintain cooperation among men should as surely destroy some men morally as battle destroys them physically. Leadership can fail because leaders can fail. (Waldo 1968, 51)

The archetype of a leader who is morally destroyed by his struggle to maintain cooperation among men is Captain Queeg in the movie *The Caine Mutiny*.

In the following chapters we will explore the manner that movie stories, we can call them cases if you like, explore conflict between the organization and its members.

Chapter Three

Fragility of Harmony: The Case of *Network*

" Here's a Howdy Do! Here's a pretty mess!"
The Mikado, Gilbert and Sullivan

The movie *Network* draws a diagram of a modern organization infused with disharmony. It sets the scene for more detailed observations that will be made in subsequent chapters. In this film we observe an organizational sea where the fish swim in currents and counter currents of omnipresent conflicting values and interests. There is no better illustration of the fragility of organizational harmony and the way that this can result in the illusiveness of human happiness.

The text of Network, the story that it tells, is a compelling criticism of the way that television displaces individuality and freedom with an overpowering mass culture. The perpetrator of wrongdoing in the story is the tube and the victim is the passive audience that accepts what comes over the tube as truth. On the other hand, the context of the story, its circumstance, reveals the culprit to be the organizations that produce and deliver television programs; in the circumstance described the villain is the network and its corporate masters.

The victims caught up in the circumstance portrayed by this movie are the people who have the job of delivering the revelations of a false god, TV, to attract, even seduce, viewers. The tragic mechanism is the ratings system and the quest for the audience approval that determines network profit. In the final analysis, the victim of the media of television is the audience and the casualty is human truth; the victims of the organization are its members and the casualty here is human happiness.

Organizations as systems of cooperation for a purpose have both an anatomy and a physiology. The anatomy describes the structure of the organizational design, its arrangements, its rules, its procedures. Sometimes we find it useful to call this the formal organization. This is the diagram of the organization in the same way that a picture of skeleton, muscle, blood vessels, etc. is a picture of the human anatomy.

The physiology of an organization describes its processes: the ebb and flow of human decisions and behavior that constitutes the action and interaction among all the elements of the organizational body. We often refer to this as the informal organization.

Of course, neither the formal structure nor the informal process of behavior operate in a vacuum. They interact. The existence, for example, of a formal hierarchy and of the mandate to increase the program ratings influences the state of mind and the behavior of the organization's members. Similarly, the formal structure of the organization is adjusted in response to employee behavior. When, for instance, employees are motivated by the values of the journalist's profession and when this has a negative impact on program ratings and profits, we will see that the organization adjusts its structure to weaken the influence of those who attempt to maintain professional values rather than those values that maximize profit.

At times, conflict between the organization's quest for formal goals and the aspirations of employees can result in a mixture of structure and process that is pathological; the organizational system and its parts can become diseased.

To understand the pathology of an organization we need to look at both its anatomy and its physiology. Let's start with anatomy. The organizational diagram revealed in the movie *Network* is a complex mélange of hierarchal relationships among corporations and individuals.

At the very bottom we have the News Division of UBS Network. The News Division is unique. It is not a profit center. Other divisions of UBS Network report to the network leadership. The News Division reports directly to corporate headquarters (UBS Systems). Other divisions are considered to be profit centers and are held responsible by UBS network executives for the ratings that result in profit (or loss). The News Division is free of this constraint. The intent of this design is that delivering the news will be a public service that relies on the professionalism of journalists as a driving force rather than on the shifting winds of public taste, sponsor influence and program popularity. This is an unambiguous example of a structure designed to encourage desired behavior, i.e. the creation of news programming the purpose of which is to inform and enlighten the audience rather than to seduce their passive viewing.

The central characters that inhabit the News Division are two accomplished middle-aged professionals. Max Schumaker leads the division. Howard Beale is the evening news anchorman. Max and Howard are longtime friends who entered their profession at the earliest, and for them the happiest, days of television news broadcasting. The arrangements that enable the News Division to operate independent of a profit motive are well suited to both Max and Howard's professional ethics.

The Programming Division of the network does report to network leadership and is responsible for the production of the high audience viewer ratings that result in profit. Programming is under the direction of the Vice President for Programming, Diana Christianson, a young, attractive, upwardly mobile, ambitious (even ruthless) executive. Independence from the ratings system and the profit motive is anathema to Diana. She craves the pursuit of ratings and profit. She is therefore not at all pleased with the concept of a professionally run News Division. It insults her corporate executive ethics.

The UBS network is under the control of UBS Systems, a large communication corporation that owns a wide variety of media subsidiaries operating in TV, radio, magazines etc. This corporation is under the direction of Frank Hackett. Hackett has become increasingly involved in the detailed operations of UBS. As the story unwinds, UBS Systems is acquired by CCA (Communications Corporation of America) which is in turn absorbed by WWF (World Wide Funding), a holding company of global dimensions. The Chairman of WWF is Mr. Jensen.

The formal arrangements here are not just a hierarchical arrangement of the players in the game. They are also a ladder of organizations, each of which controls the destiny of the corporate systems and people below. The higher level organization, e.g. CCA or WWF, or the higher level leader, e.g. Frank Hackett or Mr. Jensen, may attempt to optimize higher level aspirations and at the same time degrade (suboptimize) outcomes for the systems and people at a lower level. When we look at the organizations that are held by other corporations in what is formally one mega-conglomeration, the whole does not necessarily equal the sum of the parts. The interest of the whole and the interests of the parts can be in conflict. In this story they are in conflict.

The clash of interest exists from bottom to top. Howard and Max (in the News Division of UBS) are motivated to inform the audience of the truth. Diana (in the Programming Department of UBS) is motivated by ratings. Frank Hackett (of UBS Systems and CCA) is motivated by profit. And Mr. Jensen (at WWF) is motivated by an ideology of the globalization of business, having nothing to do with either profits, per se, or truth. Given that each actor in the drama acts in his own self interest, the structure contains the seeds for conflict, discontent, misery and worse.

Now that we have set the stage by describing the anatomy of organizational arrangement and the players, we can push the start button and observe the physiology, the process that unwinds.

At the start of the story Howard Beale is a mandarin of TV. His fortunes, however, both personal and professional, are on the decline. His wife has died, his youth has faded and the ratings of his show are declining. He is morose. He drinks heavily. As a result of poor audience ratings, Howard is fired. He commiserates with Max and they recall the old days when

Fragility of Harmony

they worked for NBC and CBS news. These were the days when TV news was in its infancy and the profit making power of TV had not been revealed. Howard and Max could therefore conform to professional ethics and be happy with their organizational roles. But the times, they are changing. Ratings now rule the organizational roost.

Howard reacts to hard times by announcing on the air that "... his show is the only thing I had going for me in my life. I am going to blow my brains out right on this program, a week from now...We ought to get a helluva rating out of that."

Max, who is Howard's boss as well as his friend, argues sarcastically that TV audiences will welcome the sight of Howard's suicide. Max jokingly fantasizes about a program called suicide of the week that will blow "...that fucking Disney right off the air."

Up to this point in his organizational life, Howard has had no problem reconciling his public and his private persona. What he *did*, news broadcasting, and what he *was*, a professional journalist, were well integrated. But this sense of inner harmony has been destroyed and he has publicly announced the very private decision to take his own life.

Meanwhile, Frank Hackett is getting ready for a UBS Systems stock holders meeting where he will announce a restructuring plan. Hackett sees an opportunity to increase profitability by changing the status and the purpose of the network's News Division. He points out to Max that he has "...had it up to here with your News Division and its annual 33 million dollar deficit." Hackett wants to convert the News Division into a profit center and make it responsible to the network for high ratings. This in turn will increase Hackett's usefulness to the Systems corporation and increase his own power.

Hackett's plan is anathema to Max. It will drastically change his division's professional approach to news programming as well as emasculate the personal and professional power of Max. "You keep your hands off my News Division, Frank," proclaims Max. There is now conflict of principle and of person. The professionalism of the journalist, Max, clashes with the profit ethic of the corporate executive, Hackett.

Superimposed on this is the personal power struggle between the egos of two human beings who might as well be members of two distinct species.

In the midst of this conflict and struggle, Frank Hackett finds a valuable ally in Diana Christianson. Both Hackett and Diana want to ride the magic carpet of ratings to personal success. Diana's move in the chess game of corporate power plays is to develop a program that encourages a politically radical group, the Ecumenical Liberation Army, to film their participation in bank robberies, and to make these films the basis of a TV show. She sees the TV audience as bored and seeks to exploit what she calls "the popular rage." As she views the "home movie" of a bank robbery she says, "This is terrific stuff, I think we can get a movie of the week out of it...maybe even a series." Such an idea is repellant to the professional ethics of both Howard and Max.

While Hackett and Diana plan their own strategies for change, Howard decides he would "like another shot." "I don't want to go out like a clown," he protests to Max. Max allows Howard to go on. This is Howard's last broadcast and he has promised to act in a restrained manner. But Howard can no longer conform to professional or industry standards. He tells his audience that he is leaving his job because he "just ran out of bullshit!" Howard has become a rebel. His behavior conforms neither to the professional standards of Max nor the profit standards of Hackett.

At the meeting he has been so carefully preparing for, Hackett informs the stockholders that the "business of management is management." He announces his restructuring plan, a plan that eliminates the discretion of the network News Division. Furthermore, he tells the stockholders that CCA has taken control of UBS and that this move is part of a plan for the "coordination of the main profit centers." His intention is to make each division more "responsive to management." He says that historically News Divisions are expected to lose money and that will be changed. Hackett and Max are now full-blown enemies.

Max was not told about Hackett's plan. He feels publicly humiliated in front of the stockholders. Max is resentful and alienated from the organization. Rather than cut Howard off the air as Howard announces that he has "run out of bullshit," Max agrees with Howard. "He is saying that life is bullshit...so what are you screaming about?" Max asks the shocked crew in the news program control booth. Hackett tries to intervene by ordering Max, via a phone call, to cut Howard off the air. Max rebels. "Leave him on," he proclaims. "Tell Mr. Hackett to go fuck himself." Max is shedding his professional mantel for that of a much more complex and problematic human persona.

The Network President, George Ruddy, fires Max for letting Howard continue on the air. He is the man in the middle between Hackett and Max. Ruddy admires Max and despises Hackett, but he is powerless in this situation. Hackett's influence at UBS Systems and at CCA has emasculated the man at the top of the UBS network.

Diana sees Howard's rebellion and his troubles as an opportunity. She convinces Hackett to use Howard to increase ratings. She wants to "articulate the popular rage" and sees Howard's personal range as the means to do this. But Howard works for the News Division and she has no control over news programming. She makes her first power play move on Hackett. "I want that show, Frank," she tells Hackett. Hackett makes the point that using Howard as a clown-newscaster is too unconventional. Yet both Hackett and Diana agree that putting a manifestly irresponsible man on television is not such a bad idea. The more Howard acts irresponsibly on the air, they believe, the more the audience will be attracted to him.

Max accepts his demise at the network and decides that he may teach or do, "what ever one does in the autumn of ones years." His crisis on the job has precipitated a personal crisis: the realization that he is in his sunset years and that he is "closer the end than to the beginning." He is no longer able to integrate the public and the private elements of his life. Up to now his power on the job has masked his declining personal vitality. But the mask has been removed as a result of the scheming of Hackett.

Now under the influence of Diana, Hackett wants to put Howard on the air to do his "angry man thing as a latter day prophet denouncing the hippocracies of our time." There is agreement among those at the News Division that they will refuse to allow that to happen. His colleagues want to support Howard and help to prevent him from being used. Howard, however, is in danger of leading a completely empty life. He tells his colleagues, "Wait a minute. That's my job you're tuning down." Howard decides to accept Hackett's offer. By doing so he becomes a willing pawn in the power game. Howard's ego needs to be fed by whatever scraps are available at the network. There is simply no other source of satisfaction for him. He has become, in effect, the willing slave of the people and the values that in better days he abhorred.

The network President is shocked at Hackett's and Diana's idea of electronic tabloid journalism. But Ruddy believes that CCA executives will be upset at Hackett's presumptuousness and that Mr.Jensen, who sits at the very top of the corporate pyramid, will be distressed. He asks Max to stay on the job. Like Howard, Max is reluctant to detach himself from a working environment of a lifetime. He needs the corporate crutch a little longer. He stays on.

The novelty of Howard as an angry prophet wears off and the initial high ratings of the new show decline. This presents Diana with an opportunity to grab the golden ring. She seduces Max, both personally and professionally. First of all they become lovers. Max is reacting to the onset of male menopause. The stress he experiences causes him to escape into a relationship that even he realizes can only fail. "What are you doing, schmuck?" he asks himself as he launches his affair. Diana's seduction of Max professionally is motivated by her desire to control and rescue the ratings hungry Howard Beale news hour. Max agrees that the show does need help with the ratings and Diana, by planning to sensationalize the program with spectacular showmanship, promises to make the Beale show the highest rated show in TV.

Max thinks Howard is making a fool of himself and wants to push Howard back to the traditional news format. Diana tells Max that sooner or later, she is going to take over his network news show. Diana's appeal as a sex object and a means for him recover his lost youth has become a way for Max to escape his personal reality. He clings desperately, however, to the last vestiges of his professional reality.

Max removes Howard's angry screwball show from the air. Howard is to do the news in a conventional manner. But when Howard abandons the prepared news script and starts to tell the audience on yet another final show that he is hearing voices in the night that anoint him and appoint him to deliver an important message, Max lets him finish. Howard says that the voice wants him to tell the people the truth.

In a vain attempt to maintain his own integrity, Max cancels Howard's show. He thinks Howard is having a breakdown. Hackett tells Max that Howard has been a smash hit with the viewing public. Hackett wants him on the air. Max thinks that taking on the role of a mad prophet will destroy Howard. The show is taken away from Max and given to Diana. Now Diana's professional seduction of Max is complete.

Ruddy, the C.E.O., has had a heart attack and dies. Hackett takes Ruddy's place and fires Max. Hackett is now unambiguously in control of the network. His success is punctuated by the skyrocketing ratings of the Beale (screwball) news hour.

Now Hackett has a hit show. He is going to announce higher earnings to the CCA board. Diana goes along with this. Max says to Diana, "Well, lets say fuck you too honey." Max has let go of both of his life rafts, the young and attractive Diana, and his job at the network. For Diana, however, there is no distinction at all between her public life and her private life. In fact, the latter is merely a means to enhance the former.

Howard Beale goes on TV with the comment, "I must make my witness." He announces that "Everybody knows things are bad... the dollar buys a nickel's worth...punks are running wild in the streets... the air is unfit to breath... the world we're living in is growing smaller...I want you to get mad...You have got to say, 'I am a human being, my life has value.' I want all of you to get up right now and go to the window and yell, 'I'm as mad as hell and I'm not going to take this any more'."

The result is that people all over the country do exactly as Howard asks. When Diana hears of this she says, "Sonofa bitch, we struck the mother lode!"

The Beale show becomes the top ratings show in news and the fourth best in all TV. Inspired and encouraged by this success, Diana goes to California to set up a reality TV show with the Ecumenical Liberation Army. The show is the *Mao Tse-Tung Hour*.

Frank Hackett becomes Chairman of CCA. Howard, in one of his more idealistic moods, is shocked by this. He decides to undermine Hackett's career. He tells his audience that "We are in the boredom killing business. So turn off your TV sets and leave them off." Hackett has risen to great heights on the back of viewer willingness to watch UBS shows. And Howard is telling the people to turn off their sets.

Hackett reports profit success due to the ratings of the Beale show. Mr. Jensen, now sitting as the head of World Wide Funding, says, "Very good Frank...exemplary...Keep it up."

Max retires and eventually resumes his affair with Diana. His state of mind is revealed when he tells her that, "All my friends are either dying or having grandchildren." He needs the reassurance of Diana's physical love.

Diana and Max go off for a romantic weekend, but all she can do is talk about her job, even while having sex. During afterglow of lovemaking she tells Max that she is thinking of doing a homosexual soap opera. The conflict between Diana and Max exists on many levels. The most visible conflict results from the fact that at this point in his life, the only thing that matters to Max is his private self. And the only thing that matters to Diana is her public self.

Max tells his wife about his affair with Diana and informs her that, "I don't know how I feel...But I am grateful that I can feel anything." His wife asks him to leave and he moves in with Diana.

Diana's reality TV program, the *Mao Tse-Tung Hour*, continues on the air. The radical leaders of the Liberation Army become capitalists, interested more in profit, syndication, and subsidiary rights than political reform. Ironically, as long as the radicals were ideological purists, robbing banks and committing other crimes against a society that they hate, their interest and the interest of the corporation executives coincided. They committed crimes that fascinated the TV audience. And the corporation made money. But as the radicals learn to enjoy the taste of big money, they become players and therefore competitors with the executive/capitalists in the big money game. The conflict of principles: journalism vs. sensationalism or radical socialism vs.capitalism, has become a pure struggle for power, personal gain and corporate profit.

At a meeting of network affiliate stations, Diana gives a triumphant speech. She is now famous as the woman behind the highly rated Howard Beale show. Howard, however, throws water on the flaming ambition of both Diana and Hackett. He informs his audience that Western World Funding Corporation is buying CCA for somebody else, the Arabs. Apparently, Howard is upsetting the apple cart of Mr.Jensen, who is at the head of WWF. Jensen becomes upset when Howard rages on, telling how the Arabs are buying up the U.S. Howard criticizes the CCA deal because foreign ownership of American assets is is ruining the American economy. He tells his audience to telegram the White House and say, " 'I'm as mad as hell and I'm not going to take it anymore...I want the CCA deal stopped now'."

Hackett and Diana, as well as other corporate executives, put their heads together. Frank tells them that CCA has $2 billion in loans with the Saudis and Howard has blown the whistle on the influx of Arab money. "We need that Saudi money, bad," Hackett informs them. "That show was a disaster..a death knell...I'm dead...I'm finished". The White House is knee-deep in telegrams. Hackett agonizes, "Four hours ago I was a sun god at CCA. Now I'm a man without a corporation."

Mr. Jensen calls Howard to the WWF boardroom for a face-to-face confrontation. He forcefully lectures Howard:

> You have meddled with the primal forces of nature and I won't have it. The Arabs have taken billions and now they must put it back... here are no nations, no peoples, there is only one holistic system of systems...multinational dominion of dollars...petrodollars, marks, francs, shekels, yen...It is the international system of currency that determines... the natural order of things on this planet today...And you have meddled with the primal forces of nature. And you will atone!
>
> There is no America, no democracy, only IBM, ITT, Union Carbide, Exxon etc. Those are the nations today. The world is a college of corporations determined by the immutable bylaws of business. The world is a business. It has been since man crawled out of the slime. Our children will live to see that perfect world in which there is no war or famine, oppression or brutality, one vast and ecumenical holding company where all work to share common profit, all necessities provided, all boredom amused. And I have chosen you to preach this.

When Howard asks, "Why me?" Mr. Jensen replies, "Because you're on TV, dummy."

Now UBS is presented with a severe problem. Mr. Jensen wants to keep Howard Beale on the air. He wants Howard to preach the corporate cosmology he has so carefully explained. He wants to use the network for propaganda rather than profit.

Howard tells his viewers that democracy is a dying giant and that individual freedom is finished. That is exactly the message that Mr. Jensen wants him to deliver. Howard's new theme is that dehumanization might not be so bad after all. This is a depressing argument. Nobody wants to hear that his life is valueless and the ratings of the show dip significantly.

With low ratings, the power position of Diana and Hackett becomes fragile. Diana cannot find a replacement for Howard, but she needs to fire him to improve the ratings. At the same time Hackett knows that Mr. Jensen has taken a strong personal interest in the Beale show. If Howard stays on the air, UBS and CCA profits will decline. But Hackett cannot fire Howard because Howard has the support of the man at the top.

UBS and CCA executives meet and decide that the only solution to this problem is to assassinate Howard Beale. Mr.Jensen thinks Beale delivers an important message. He does not care if the Beale show loses money and he will not allow Beale to be fired.

At the start of the story it was not important that the network News Division lost money. The reason was that the professional ideology of journalism needed to be protected. Now it matters not, at least to Jensen, that the entire network loses money. And the reason is that the ideology of globalization needs to be nurtured. The initial, as well as the final, conflict in the movie is the clash of profit and principle.

This clash transposes itself into conflict between and among people. Diana believes that if they get rid of Howard, they can recover ratings. Short of that,UBS stands to lose $45 million. Hackett agrees. He tells the assembled executives, "I suppose we'll have to kill him." Diana agrees to get the Liberation Army rebels/capitalists to do it on the show.

Howard Beale is assassinated on the air. The movie ends with a comment from an unseen narrator: "Thus Howard Beale was the first man who was killed because he had lousy ratings."

Chapter Four

Complexity of Purpose: The Case of *Twelve O'clock High*

> "Thus, in the shadow of organization we find all the repressed opposites of rationality struggling to surface and change the nature of rationality in practice...The more the bureaucratic form of organization advances the more perfectly it succeeds in eliminating all human qualities that escape technical calculation." *Images of Organization,* Gareth Morgan,

Network tells a story of ubiquitous conflict. Ubiquitous conflict is nothing new. The Seventeenth Century philosopher Thomas Hobbes observed that life is a war of all against all. Without some intrusive control of the individual, Hobbes said, "... the life of man is solitary, poor, nasty, brutish and short." Hobbes saw the powerful leviathan-like state as the cure for chaos. (Hobbes 1982) Since Hobbes' time, a predominant mechanism of intrusive control devised to help us progress from chaos to order is the modern organization.

Max Weber discerned that modern systems of organization have one common characteristic: the bureaucratic form. Rules, standard procedures, hierarchal ladders of authority and the division of labor among specialists (Weber 1946) comprise the basic anatomy of today's organizations, both public and private.

The bureaucratic promise is that the mayhem of the streets will be moderated by police departments, international anarchy mitigated by peacekeeping military units under the command of national security departments and of the United Nations (organization), that health will be delivered by health maintenance organizations, enlightenment and discovery produced by the university, salvation will become the yield of a Church, and economic security and material well being provided by the corporation. Yet the very instruments that are designed to help bring all of us out of a condition of irrational chaos and into a world of rationality and order are often sources of unhappiness for many who participate in the activities of organizations.

It is virtually impossible to live in the modern world without participating in the activity of the generic organization. We depend on the vigor of organizations. We are the beneficiaries of private and public bureaucracy. We are also its victims. The life force of many people is devoted primarily, if not exclusively, to performing an organizational role. Such immersion inevitably results in the stress generated by simultaneous reward and penalty. Many find that the organizational aspect of their lives is a mixed blessing, one which they cannot live with and cannot live without. It does not take much of an imagination to conceive of an organization that is working, but is not working for you. The Hobbesian image of a solitary, poor, nasty and brutish existence, when transposed to the context of organizational life, as in the film story *Network*, can expose an unhappy reality. Why is this so?

An inherent and fundamental condition of organizational life is that the interests of the organization as a whole and the interests of the members of the organization and the interest of the constituency of the organization (clients and customers) are not necessarily the same. The idea that enables us to start to understand this condition is the concept of purpose.

Before we get into definitions and analysis of what is involved in unpacking the notion of purpose, let's start by looking at the story told by the film *Twelve O'clock High*. Stories about military organizations are the most common form taken by the Legend of the Dysfunctional System. There is an important message here for those who would learn from the Legend. The military unit is a useful metaphor for any organization because organizations are potential fields of "combat" and because the military situation, at least during a war, is often less ambiguous (with respect to what the organization is trying to accomplish) than other sorts of organizations. Gordon Geko, in the movie *Wall Street*, is the quintessential modern executive. The bible that guides his organizational strategy has not to do with concepts of capitalism or management. Geko's bible is *The Art of War* authored by the ancient Chinese military strategist, Sun Tsu.

The *Twelve O'clock High* film story, which is in many respects a docudrama of historical events, takes place in the early years of U.S. involvement in World War II. U.S. leaders have decided to dedicate the Army's emerging aviation assets, organized into the form of the Army Air Corps, to daylight precision bombing of enemy targets in Europe. In daylight, accuracy of bombing will be greater than at night. The decision to fly bombing missions in daylight, however, presents some significant problems. First of all, bombing enemy targets in daylight is a very risky business because the bombers are vulnerable to enemy ground fire and fighter attack. For this reason the British strategic doctrine calls for the blanket bombing of cities and enemy installations at night.

A second problem is that the U.S. is unprepared for its entry into the war. The American war machine has not yet come up to speed. There is a critical shortage of planes, in particular the B-17 Flying Fortresses that would be used for the daylight bombing mission. And there is a shortage of trained crews. In a characteristic display of self-confidence, American leaders decide to muddle through until sufficient planes can be built and sufficient crews trained.

The organization that is the focus of the story is the 918th Bomber Group. In many respects this group, and others like it, are the guinea pigs that will test the concept of daylight precision bombing and at the same time hold the fort until the U.S. can mobilize its manpower and industrial strength.

Based in England, the 918th consists of a number of squadrons that put up 20 or more aircraft each time

Headquarters calls for a bombing mission, first against German targets in France and later against targets in the German homeland itself.

The Commanding Officer of the group, Colonel Keith Davenport, has great empathy for the crews of his planes. The 918th seems to be a "hard luck" group, losing men and machines to enemy action at an alarming rate. The situation is particularly grim because there are no relief crews on the horizon. The crews on scene will probably just keep flying until they fall victim to enemy action. "These boys can count," states Davenport. "They know they don't have a chance!"

The group is ordered to fly at lower altitudes to make their bombing more accurate. Davenport objects strenuously. He points out to his bosses at headquarters that the lower altitude will make his crews even more vulnerable to enemy antiaircraft fire. When one of his navigators is chided by higher command for making costly errors, Davenport refuses to relieve the young officer of his navigation duties. General Pritchard, the leader of all the groups in England, is certain that Davenport has fallen victim to over-identification with his men and is no longer an effective group commander. Pritchard removes Davenport from his command position and taps General Frank Savage to shape up the 918th.

Savage is a dedicated professional who sees his leadership task as taking a hard-nosed attitude. He gives the men a reality check by telling them that they "...have to fight because they are in a war, a shooting war, and some are going to have to die." He advises them that "It is O.K. to be afraid," but they should "ignore that fear" and "consider themselves to be already dead." He challenges "anyone who is not man enough" to follow his suggestion to request a transfer from the group. The men unanimously opt for a transfer.

Aided by a loyal ground officer, Major Harvey Stoval, Savage manages to delay the written transfer requests of his aircrews. He uses the time to improve the technical skills of the crews and to develop some pride in his followers. Savage successfully solicits the cooperation of one of the youngest and most admired pilots, Lieutenant Jessie Bishop. When

Bishop withdraws his request for transfer, so do the rest of the men.

Now the 918th really gets to work and starts making a useful contribution to the war effort. The odds against individual survival, however, remain high, and as Savage leads the group he loses many of his men. Although Savage does not consciously or openly admit it, these men have become his comrades in arms. He empathizes with them. But he controls his feelings because he believes the group needs a harsh task master. Savage never lets his guard down. Acting the hard-nosed leader has worked for him and he continues to maintain that posture. As a result, he ends his tour as commander of the 918th with a nervous breakdown. His attempt to bottle up his feelings for his men has had a toll on his own mental stability. Savage has becomes a victim of the war and has learned the limits of his own humanity.

How can this story help us understand the idea of purpose and enable us to discern the basis of the Legend of the Dysfunctional System?

As we view the story, we are presented with a description of a situation, with the facts of the story. Organizations indeed are entities that can be described by facts. The job descriptions of members, the assets and liabilities, the rules and regulations, the policy and procedures and the ladder of authority are all factual constructs. Certainly, General Savage is a stickler for the formal (fact of life) rules. When an enlisted clerk is observed to be out of uniform he reduces him in rank from Sergeant to Private. When a senior pilot, Lieutenant Colonel Ben Gaitley, leaves the base and gets drunk during the crisis of Davenport's dismissal, Savage removes him from his position in the hierarchy and assigns him as pilot of a crew filled with misfits to fly a plane that Savage names "The Leper Colony." The structure of the organization, its anatomy, is described in factual terms.

The decisions that formulate the day-to-day activity of the organization, its processes, its physiology, are based, at least in part, on factual premises. If the planes fly at 9000 feet of altitude they will destroy more targets than if they fly at 19,000 feet. The decision to lower the standard bombing altitude is based on this factual premise.

But organizations are not just machine-like producers of action based on a factual rationality. They are also institutions, i.e. complex social systems with deeply infused values. The complex melange of values that define the soul of the organization represents a chain of means and ends that winds up identifying the highest or end game value of the organized system. This end game value expresses the formal purpose of the organization.

In Twelve O'clock High, the lives of the aircrews express a valued entity, just as the skills of the fliers are a factual element. Technology and tactics are designed to help the pilots stay alive and do their jobs. Yet the aircrews and their skills are not an end in and of themselves. They are a means to achieving the objective of destroyed enemy targets, a valued goal. And the destroyed targets are a means to achieving the valued end of winning the war. So we might say that the purpose of the 918th is winning the war. And that is true. But that notion leaves out as much as it puts in. It only explains part of what is going on.

One reason that organizations often seem, at least potentially, to be so imperfect or dysfunctional, is that in reality there is more than one governing purpose for which organizations exist, not just the one explicitly expressed by the formal purpose (i.e.mission). If a person from Mars were asked to observe organizational life and speculate on the purpose for the existence of modern organizations, the predominant social structure with which earthlings get things done, he or she (or it) would conclude that there are three purposes. Only one of the three purposes is written into policy or into the organization manual: the formally stated mission. The other two can be inferred, as would the Martian, by watching the behavior of the organized system and its parts.

The first, and most obvious, purpose is the formal mission, the delivery of some goods or services to a client, customer, or constituency. For the 918th Bomber Group this is helping to win the war for the American people.

Complexity of Purpose

Yet there are times, as we observe the way the organizational process proceeds, as we examine the criteria that leaders and followers use for making decisions, that the purpose (end game value in the chain of means and ends) appears to be satisfaction of the needs of individual participants. Of course, everybody wants to win the war. But as these men try to do so, all the aircrews are going to lose their lives. Because of this the leader, Colonel Keith Davenport, designs the organization and runs it so that the crews survive (purpose), rather than that the war is won. His decision to object to flying at a lower altitude is a demonstration of the value premise behind that decision. Similarly, Colonel Davenport's decision to refuse to fire the weak navigator is based on the young man's very strong need to prove himself to be a loyal American even though his parents are German immigrants. The value premise of decisions made by Colonel Davenport consists of the value of preserving the lives and dignity of the aircrews. This is in conflict with the factual premise of headquarters that flying lower will result in the destruction of more targets as well as the factual premise that there are plenty of trained proficient navigators. So we have the purpose of the organization, as expressed in the logic of the mission, in conflict with the purpose of the individual participant, to stay alive or to have his patriotism validated. If the organization is functional with respect to destroying enemy targets, it is dysfunctional with respect to preserving the lives of its members, and visa versa.

Organizations are systems of cooperation for rational action. The idea of rational, however, does not prescribe objective criteria for evaluating or predicting behavior. Rational means the optimization of some value. I drive a large pick up truck because I want to optimize the value of the capacity to tow my horses around the countryside. My wife drives a small 4 cylinder import because she wants to optimize the value of fuel economy. Both behaviors are rational because they result in an outcome that the decision maker finds useful.

General Savage wants to optimize the value of targets destroyed. For Colonel Davenport and for the young men who fly the aircraft of the 918th, the value to be optimized is the survival of aircrews.

It is important to understand that organizations do not generally come into existence to serve the needs of participants. It is assumed that the members of the organization will serve a purpose derived from the original design of the organization. And that assumption is generally true, albeit an oversimplification of complex reality. The assumption is rarely true in the absolute. Whether or not the purpose of serving the needs of members, when those needs come into conflict with the formal purpose of the organization, is legitimate or is pathological is a matter of philosophy and politics. In a socialistic political-economic system, the responsibility of institutions, both private and public, includes the nurturing of participants, perhaps to an extent above and beyond the straight forward exchange of labor for benefit. Here the dominance of the purpose of the individual might not be considered so irrational or pathological. Indeed, in the early days of the birth of a welfare state in the U.S, the federal government formed organizations (such as the WPA) designed almost exclusively to serve the individual necessity of employees. In a free market capitalistic system, however, the benefits provided to the participants are believed to be in exchange for services that accomplish a mission. Nurturing the individual just for his own sake would not be considered rational.

Rationality and pathology notwithstanding, even in capitalistic nations people do behave as though the organization should exist, at least in part, to serve their particular interests. In explaining this notion to my students, I tell them that the college I work for exists, at least in part, to give me something to do when I wake up in the morning. Of course my students react to this rather glib statement by concluding that my tongue is firmly placed inside my cheek. This is not the case. If I believe that the relationship between me and my organization is based solely on the way I serve the more narrow rationality of the organization, I am vulnerable to perceiving myself as a tool in the hands of another. Because the hand that holds the tool also controls the tool this might be the first step on the road giving up responsibility for my own happiness. Philosophically, at least for me, the sanctity of the individual person, the well being of his mind, body and soul, mitigates toward giving him the benefit of the doubt when, from time to time, he seems to be using the organization to a greater extent than the organization is using him.

A third operative purpose is the survival and health of the organization itself. One of the problems faced by the 918th Bomber Group is that the tactic of daylight precision bombing is experimental and believed by many, the British and the ground forces of the U.S. Army in particular, to be too risky and non-productive. The Army Air Corps is a relatively new organization. The willingness of American political and military leaders to devote scarce material and manpower to this organization, indeed to allow its continued existence, depends on the Corps' capacity to demonstrate that it can help win the war with daylight precision bombing. So, at times we see that the value premise of decisions optimizes the continued existence (survival) as an institution, and the continued resource support (health) of the Army Air Corps.

The personification of this phenomenon is the General who leads the 8th Airforce, of which the 918th is part, General Pritchard. He tells the new leader of the group, General Savage, that his men must fly at lower altitudes and destroy more targets even though this means they may all be killed before they get relieved by other crews now in training. A sensible strategy might be to hold off and wait until they have enough crews and planes to let each crew fly a specified number of missions and then go home. This would motivate the men because they would expect the satisfaction of accomplishing a meaningful goal, the preservation of their lives. This is coming soon and this is what eventually happens. But Pritchard expresses his fears that if the Army Air Corps does not press on despite horrendous losses, daylight precision bombing will be discredited. And that might mean the end of organizations like the 918th and perhaps of the Army Air Corps whose essence is strategic bombing. Of course, General Pritchard wants to win the war. And he would prefer that the aircrews survive. But for a time he acts as though his highest value is the survival and health of the 918th and the Army Air Corps.

In the ideal, the three purposes: mission, self, and institutional health and survival, are not in conflict. In this story, one of the most important functions of the leader is to integrate the divergent purposes. The new leader of the 918th, General Savage (the hero of the story), figures out a way to do this, albeit at great cost to his own mental health and at great loss of the life of the aircrews. Savage convinces the aircrews that placing bombs on target and the contribution of this to the war effort is more important to them, as individuals, than is their own lives. When his advice to the men to "...consider themselves already dead," results in massive resignations from a voluntary flying status, Savage focuses on a young pilot who, by virtue of his heroism and stoicism, is respected by all aircrewmen. The General tells Lieutenant Bishop that "...a man has to decide for himself." Bishop needs, more than anything else, to confirm his status as a man. But to do so he must realign his values in an extreme way. He has to accept the proposition that the value of placing bombs on German targets is greater than the value of his own life. And this he does. General Savage gets Lieutenant Bishop and the others to replace their instinctive purpose (staying alive) with a societal purpose (winning the war).

The way General Savage convinces Lieutenant Bishop to give up his life for a cause takes advantage of Bishop's vanity. This seems reasonable, albeit sad, to an audience that values the cause.

But the cause is not always universally and unambiguously admirable. In the movie *Devil's Advocate*, the Devil in the form of the senior partner (Milton) in a law firm, takes advantage of a young lawyer's (Lomax) vanity to gain control of his soul. Both Bishop in *Twelve O'clock High* and Lomax in *Devil's Advocate* have free will. But their freedom is limited by the willingness, indeed the necessity, of the leader to push the goals of the organization against the interest of the lower level participant. "Vanity is my favorite sin," proclaims the Devil (as Milton). The vanity of his pilots, their need to act like real men, is also General Savage's favorite sin. The viewer may conclude that Savage is good and Milton is evil. The form of the two stories is different. But the message is the same: The human being is potentially a victim of the organizational machine. This is the essence of the Legend of the Dysfunctional System.

Chapter Five

The Problem of Multiple Roles: The Cases of *Electric Horseman, In Pursuit of Honor, Lost in America*

> "...The souls of horses mirror the souls of men more closely than men suppose...But no creature can learn that which his heart has no shape to hold...If a person understood the soul of a horse then he would understand all horses that ever were."
> *All The Pretty Horses,* Cormac McCarthy,

The fundamental cause of the vulnerability of participants to organizational forces is the complexity of purpose that we find in the organization's environment. But the vulnerability of the individual to conflicting purposes is only a condition of potential pain. When does this potential become real distress for the individual?

For an organization to function at all, leaders must send a message to followers concerning not only what the follower should *do*, but, more important, what the follower should *be*. General Savage could tell his pilots to ignore their impending death, but this directive was only a hollow imperative until he could convince them to *be* self-sacrificing heroes. General Pritchard could only get Savage to be willing to sacrifice his men in the name of victory, or in the name of the Army Air Corps, if he could get Savage to *be* an extraordinarily cold and harsh task master.

The actor who plays Lieutenant Jessie Bishop and the actor who plays General Frank Savage interpret their roles by attempting to show us what a value or a set of values might look like in the form of human behavior, human response to the situation of the story. But there is more to these roles than we can see in the obvious behavior of the actor. Underneath Bishop's act as a hero there is stress and pain. Underneath Savage's act as the leader who is impervious to the humanity of his men there is real strain. This strain causes him to snap.

To interpret a role, the actor attempts to display the values that are implicit in that role. Bishop's face shows fear. Savages body language shows gritty determination. And to do this effectively the actor must come to a profound understanding of the values of the character he is portraying. Otherwise the telling of the film story does not work.

As we act out the events that make up the story of our lives, we play the roles that are driven by our needs. Some of these needs are common to all people. Some of these are idiosyncratic to our particular selves. For the action of our lives to work, i.e. to be satisfying to ourselves, we must have a profound understanding of what we are in the first place. But unlike the actor in the film we have neither writer nor director to guide us in this difficult task. The screen writer and the director tell Gregory Peck what Savage is. For us to find out what we are, however, can be a much more tortuous process. Let's take a look at stories (first the film *Electric Horseman*) that show us what this process looks like and how a lack of self-understanding results in distress.

Sonny Steele is the Electric Horseman. His past glory as a champion rodeo cowboy has faded. He has become an aging spokesman for a corporation. He hawks breakfast cereal at shopping center promotional events and high school half-time football game shows. He has commercialized himself, become a "product". Sonny attempts to escape from the pain of the physical injuries sustained in rodeo days and the emotional pain of corporate bondage by turning to a life a booze and casual sex. Sonny has, in the words of his friend, "...lost the best part of himself."

Rising Star is a magnificent stallion whose past glory on the racetrack has also faded. Sonny and the horse come together as fellow corporate employees. The washed-out cowboy is to ride the has-been stallion in a glitzy Las Vegas review staged by the corporation to promote its product. Sonny sees that the horse has been pumped full of steroids and tranquilizers. He sees the wreck of what was the soul of the horse. He sees himself.

In a masterful display of horsemanship and equine endurance Sonny and Rising Star unite to defect from their corporate masters with: an amazing ride through a hotel casino, a wild chase by police cruisers through the streets of Las Vegas and a dash across rugged and desolate terrain. By the time Sonny and Rising Star reach a secret place populated by herds of wild horses, both the man and the stallion are ready to begin new lives. Rising Star is turned loose and is out from under the "protection" and control of man. Sonny no longer has the security of a steady job. But both horse and man are much closer to, more in harmony with, whatever is the essence of their being, the best part of themselves.

When I asked my students to think about the situation of Sonny and to answer the question, "What is his problem?" one insightful student answered, "The corporation has uncowboyed him." After some discussion the class interpreted that statement to mean that the essence of Sonny's values could be captured by the role cowboy and that his employer required him to ignore this role and play one that was antithetical to it.

The role of cowboy captures the image of the generic mythical figure that we see displayed on the screen in classic western movies. It also reveals the inner-self of Sonny, the characteristics that define what he is: a rugged individual, a man who loves the freedom of the outdoors, who dislikes actual as well as metaphoric fences, a man who is willing to take risks, a man who is fiercely loyal to friends.

The pain of failure to understand self and the epiphany of self discovery are common themes in stories about the relationship between organizations and the people who inhabit them. Often the bearer of the mandates to "know thyself" and "to thine own self be true" comes in the form of an interaction with and an empathy for another species. In the case of Sonny Steele this is a horse. This is appropriate because (so called) lower species behave as though they have a full understanding of what they are and what behavior is appropriate to their survival and happiness. The animal plays out a natural repertoire of attitude and behavior because nature "hard wires" him to play a very specific role, that of a horse. When the horse is domesticated and his human master does not take his natural role into account the horse can act in neurotic and self destructive ways.

Man, on the other hand, has the faculty of self-consciousness and free will, the power constantly to reprogram himself. Indeed the search for his authentic "program", his nature, is a central element of man's experience of life. More often than not, he finds himself pushing against his own nature, his own soul. Life for many is a process of trial and error, an attempt to find the self that is the synthesis of human nature and man made experience: the real self. Another film makes this point quite clear.

The film *In Pursuit of Honor* tells the tale of two rebellious cavalry soldiers during the Great Depression. Down and out World War I Army veterans are protesting the Government's decision to withhold promised bonuses. Sergeant Libby becomes a maverick when he refuses to use his horse to put down the protest by terrorizing his fellow soldiers. The organization has assigned him the role of policeman. The role he wants to play, a role that is more authentic for him, is that of comrade.

Lieutenant Buxton has been sent to a dead-end remote post because he struck a fellow officer who abused a horse. Libby has also been exiled to the post. In the same way that the horse was Sonny Steele's connection to his calling of cowboy, so is the horse a connection to the soldiers' identity as cavalry men. Indeed the army horses run to muster from their pasture at the sound of a bugle; the base commander refers to himself as "...an old war horse." The mutual love of horses creates a bond of friendship between Libby and Buxton and a bond between these two and the Army.

The identity of both men, the role of both men as horse soldiers is undermined when the usefulness and practicality of the cavalry horse is overcome by progress and circumstance. Budget constraints of a peacetime army, belt tightening of *The Great Depression*, and the advent of mechanized means of transport and fighting all lead to downsizing. This means destroying large numbers of horses.

We witness the machine gunning of one hundred horses. The sight revolts the viewer. It also disgusts our two heroes. The Lieutenant proclaims, "This smacks of insanity." Buxton and Libby stampede the remaining 400 horses and flee to the desert, just as Sonny Steele fled with Rising Star. The police cars in pursuit of Steele were no match for the horse. The machines of the army cannot thwart the dash of the herd for life. Neither can these machines block the soldier's escape from the insanity of the army. In the end, the rebellious soldiers and the horses make it to Canada where the 400 hundred rescued army mounts will be given to an Indian tribe.

In each of these movies, what the human and the horse does is controlled by a modern institution: the corporation, the army. The institution has become the master of the values of the individual. The men unwittingly give up part of themselves to join civilization. It is the same with the horse. But the cost of joining civilization is the destruction of whatever they are: cavalry man, cowboy, horse. Each of these identities is made up of values that suit and are in harmony with the inner man, the natural horse. Each of these identities personifies the soul, the self of the human or the creature.

In these stories, the horse helps to recreate the integrity of the man, to bring him closer to what he is. The plight of the horse informs the man that his soul is in trouble. The capacity of the horse for flight suggests the solution to the man's problem. The same substantive story is told in the film

The Horse Whisperer. Here a publishing executive and mother discovers her authentic self as she saves her daughter's horse.

Of course, the discovery of self does not depend on interaction with a horse. There are many ways that the role one plays to satisfy the purpose of the organization and the role that one plays to live a satisfactory life can come into conflict. There are many ways that this conflict can be discovered and dealt with. A story of self discovery is told in a different form in the film *Lost in America*.

David and Linda are young upwardly mobile urban dwellers in Los Angeles. He is the artistic director of an advertising firm, one of the biggest. She is a human resource manager for a department store.

David has become a candidate for promotion to Executive Vice President. He has been climbing the corporate ladder for eight years and he considers this promotion to be the jewel in his career crown. He is so sure of the promotion that he is negotiating for the purchase of a new Mercedes and has gone into escrow to purchase a luxurious home. He is plunging headlong into unexplored territory. When he complains to Linda, "Our new house will not have a tennis court!" his wife replies, "But you don't even play tennis." He responds, "If you have a tennis court, you learn." And indeed, David has much to learn, not so much about tennis as about himself and about the relationship between whatever he is and what the corporation wants him to be.

David's boss informs him that he will be assigned to the newly acquired Ford account and transferred from the home office in Los Angeles to New York. Much to David's horror David's friend is promoted to Executive Vice President. The corporation, David is told, needs his creative talent in New York.

David's disappointment is devastating. He now perceives that all of his cooperative behavior and all of the force of his creative energy, have been motivated by the anticipation of attaining the rank of Executive Vice President. Linda comments that for years he has climbed the ladder of seniority and at each step he has proclaimed that "If I just get this, everything will be all right." His track record is one of achieving career goals and setting new and higher goals. But the more he drinks of success, the thirstier he gets.

Failure to get this promotion is a rude awakening. David makes the transition from quiet discontent to noisy disappointment in his boss' office. And he does so in a very graceless way. He turns from a cooperative Dr.Jekel into a raving Mr. Hyde. Just as pent-up compassion breaks down Savage in *Twelve O'clock High*, so raging ambition destroys David's composure. He throws a temper tantrum, quits his job and is simultaneously fired.

David is now free of the shackles of corporate America. He convinces Linda to quit her job. David and Linda sell all their assets, buy a large motor home and set off to recover their souls by traveling across the country. "I want to touch an Indian," proclaims David. But rather than finding themselves they become, at least for the time being, *Lost in America*.

On their way to a journey of exploration, the couple stops off at Las Vegas to reaffirm their love by remarrying in an all night wedding chapel. They check into a hotel. During a brief farewell to what she now considers to be the false values of modern civilization, Linda, who has not yet had a chance to savor the release of a temper tantrum or a nervous breakdown, gambles away almost all the cash (the nest egg) that David and she have acquired to support their anticipated free life style. She has lived a life of pent-up aspirations that she does not understand, aspirations that she cannot articulate. When her secretary had discussed her impending move into a large and luxurious home Linda remarked, "You know, I am going to hate this house." But she does not know why. Her desire to be fulfilled is been frustrated by the fact that she has no idea at all what will make her happy. The significant stash of cash she acquired as the result of liquidating the couple's assets does not make her feel any better than she did in the first place. She justifies her seemingly irrational gambling behavior by explaining to David that poverty frees one from responsibility.

David and Linda now have just enough cash and gas to get to a trailer park in rural Arizona. Their only survival option is to find jobs. The best David can do is sign on as a crossing guard at a school where wise guy students torment him. When a city fellow drives by in a Mercedes and asks directions to Los Angeles, David asks him if he likes the car. The reply is, "What's not to like?" We see the look on David's face. "What is not to like indeed!" David can see that there is a lot to like.

The best job Linda can find is as an assistant manager in a fast food restaurant. Her boss is an enthusiastic adolescent who condescends to let David and Linda address him by his first name, Skippy. When Linda tells Skippy the french fries he is serving are not quite defrosted, Skippy sees Linda as a managerial genius. "That's quite a wife you've got there," Skippy informs David.

The humiliation of Skippy's assumption of the role of the couple's guru is the last straw. David and Linda simultaneously come to the conclusion that life in rural Arizona is not the life for them. They decide to go to New York and get back into the mainstream of young urban professionalism.

David and Linda come to the realization that what they want is what they had all along, a cosmopolitan lifestyle. Their problem was that they did not understand themselves. They had what they wanted. But they could not appreciate what they had. Getting *Lost in America* enabled them to understand their need for the comfort, prestige, and the security of economic accomplishment, a need that could only be provided in an urban corporate environment.

Sonny Steele has the same sort of experience, that of finding the best part of himself. His contact with Rising Star convinced him that his connection with the corporation disconnected what he was from what he was doing. Just as David and Linda had to get *Lost in America*, so Sonny had to lose himself in the rugged terrain between Las Vegas and the place where Rising Star was to meet a herd of wild horses.

The idea that you have to lose yourself before you can find yourself is a very old notion. This is expressed most clearly and most emphatically in the story of *Faust* and in the variations (such as the movie *Damn Yankees*) on that myth that abound in literature and film.

When David and Linda reach New York, David goes to work on the Ford account, albeit at a reduction in salary, but with medical benefits. Linda starts work for a department store and has a child. They will live much more happily ever after than they had lived before. Their experience has convinced them that what they now do in New York, which is not different from what they did in Los Angeles, is sufficiently close to what they are.

These stories demonstrate that the problems individuals face because they are cogs in the organizational machine can be associated with confusion concerning self-identity. This is the problem of role conflict.

The roles we play consist of bundles of values, each of which is aggregated in the form of a label or stereotype. The label of *mother*, for example, consists of the values of: nurturing, love, tenderness, sacrifice etc. (Of course the particular bundle of values captured by a particular label is culturally conditioned. But the ones noted here are common to most advanced societies.) The label *executive* might capture the values of: directive, analytical, objective, forceful, decisive. But a woman might find herself in the condition of motherhood and employed as an executive. The values captured by these two roles would be in conflict.

General Savages' visible self, his conscious sense of self, his ego, might be described by the bundle of values described by the role: *General*. But another bundle of values was layered deep below the surface of Savages' ego. That was the role of *father*, a role that spoke to him in tones of responsibility to care for the well being of his men (*sons*). The same sort of phenomenon can be seen in the conflict between Sonny's role of *salesman* and that of *cowboy* as well as the two cavalrymen in *In Pursuit of Honor*. Here we observe conflict between the role of *loyal soldier* and that of *horseman*.

Most of us lead complex lives, lives that require us to perform more than one role. The condition of role conflict is therefore to be expected, we might even say normal. But to live happily, or nearly so, in this normal condition requires a good deal of self-understanding. Most of us have neither the time nor the disposition to reflect on what is below the surface of our complex egos, what might be fighting to emerge in the form of our authentic selves. Sonny Steele could not live well with himself until he understood the importance of the cowboy in him. Becoming "uncowboyed" was devastating. The horse soldiers experienced a similar shock when their mounts were in danger of downsizing. David and Linda could not shed the pain of role conflict until they experienced the pain of living in a mobile home in a small town.

The Legend of the Dysfunctional System tells us that self-understanding is most often the result of a shock to our complacency, and that like Faust we may have to go through hell, we might have to take advantage of the lessons of hell, before we can experience heaven.

Chapter Six

The Problem of Isolation: The Case of *Groundhog Day*

"His own heart laughed; and that was quite enough for him."
A Christmas Carol, Charles Dickens,

In chapter five we examined the problem of role conflict and witnessed the achievement of self-discovery that is accomplished as a result of a dramatic and severe crisis, one that could hardly go unrecognized or unmanaged. Yet most of us would not deliberately place ourselves in the boots of Sonny Steele, or of the two calvarymen, or in the position of David as a crossing guard, or Linda as an assistant to Skippy. We do not search for trauma as a mechanism of self-help.

Most of us spend a great deal of thought and energy attempting to place ourselves in situations where crises never invade our working lives. A strategy of crisis avoidance, and indeed risk avoidance, seems to be rational. It is not at all apparent that going through hell can be a prescription for getting to heaven. Rather than trying to achieve a state of happiness we try to avoid unhappiness, we try to be content.

The important distinction, however, between contentment and happiness may go unnoticed. Our potential for happiness may therefore go unrecognized. We become complacent. The option of living our organizational lives in quiet desperation may be one we choose heedlessly. But quiet desperation is a fertile ground for hidden misery.

In literature, the quintessential unhappy man who suffers from and then transcends a misery that is hidden from his own perception is Charles Dickens' Scrooge. The fantasy of Scrooge's unintended examination of his own life, of his own behavior, is a story that is retold in a different, but equally fantastic, form in the film *Groundhog Day*. This story takes place on February 2, Groundhog Day, indeed during a long series of Groundhog Days. This is the day when, in Punxsatawney Pennsylvania, the groundhog Phil leaves his den. If he sees his shadow, there will be six more weeks of winter.

Phil Conners is a TV weatherman at a small station in Pittsburgh. He does not respect the low status of the organization that employs him. He brags that "There is a major network interested in me." The weatherman and his crew are leaving on assignment to cover the story of the emergence of the groundhog. The mundane nature of this assignment is not up to the level of prestige that he expects. Phil happily informs his coworkers, producer Rita and camera man Larry, that this is the last time he is going to have to do the Groundhog Festival.

The crew of three travels to Punxsatauney. Phil stays at an upscale Bed and Breakfast while producer and camera man stay at a lesser place. He justifies this by saying that "You have to keep the talent happy." This is our first hint concerning Phil's problem. He perceives that to be happy, he has to be isolated from others.

Phil is not consciously distressed. In this respect, the situation of Phil is significantly different from that of Sonny Steele. Whatever it was that made Sonny Steele unhappy was not far from the surface. That's why Sonny had to keep beating his inner-self back with numbing alcohol and distracting sex. Sonny was far from content. On the other hand, if there is a separation between what Phil is and what he does, the separation is so wide, the authentic nature of Phil buried so deeply below the surface, below his ego (his conscious sense of himself) that it remains unrecognized and unmanaged. Rita tells him "I know you're egocentric. It's your defining characteristic." Rita sees that Phil wears his ego on his sleeve. She believes that there is not much more to Phil than his display of ego.

Like Scrooge, Phil is angry with everyone; he walks around with a very large chip on his shoulder. He utters the proverbial "bah humbug" in many different forms.

It is 6AM on February 2. Phil's alarm clock radio turns on. The song is Sonny and Cher with "I Got You Babe." Phil goes downstairs to breakfast. He humiliates the innkeeper by demanding Cappuccino when she does not even know what that is. He has to settle for just a plain cup of coffee.

On the way to cover the festival, he encounters a high school chum, Ned. Ned is an insurance salesman. Phil gives Ned the brush off. Ned is just another inferior person. Phil steps in a cold puddle of ice water. He is not paying attention to anything. His mind is elsewhere. He would rather be elsewhere. He is just as mad at the place as he is at the people. At the site of the festivities, Phil joins Rita and Larry. Phil proclaims his disdain for the people of the town: "They're hicks, Rita."

At 7:29 the groundhog comes out and sees his shadow. There will be six more weeks of winter. Phil, the weatherman, has predicted milder weather. This is contrary to the groundhog's prediction.Once again the animal, the child of nature,confronts man, the child of his own capacity for self-delusion. But Phil would rather listen to himself than be the slightest bit inspired by the animal or by the myth of the animal's weather forecasting prowess.

Contrary to the weatherman's prediction, there is a blizzard. The groundhog is correct. The storm prevents the TV crew from returning to Pittsburgh. They are stuck in Punxsatawney. Phil is not in control of his circumstance. But he wants to be. He says,"I make the weather." There is something deep inside Phil that is simmering with frustration. His desire to control nature, perhaps even his own human nature, is thwarted. And his reaction to this frustration is to deny it, to push it as far below the surface of his consciousness as he can.

It is 6AM, and it should be the next day. Phil's alarm radio goes off. Once again we hear the refrain of "I Got You Babe." The exact same scenario as the previous day is replayed: the humiliation of the innkeeper, the brush off of his high school chum. It is still the same day! Phil is aware that he is repeating the same day, but none of the other characters are cognizant of this. Just as Scrooge had to relive a portion of his previous Christmases, so Phil now relives the same Groundhog Day...over and over and over again.

Phil attempts to cope with the anxiety and unpleasantness of the repeated day by recalling a great day he had on vacation in the Virgin Islands. That was like the Garden of Eden. He relaxed. He made love. "Why couldn't I get *that* day over?" he asks. Phil is locked in his job and his lifestyle, locked in a state of quiet desperation, in a state of hidden misery. We have already witnessed the anger that reveals this. Now we see another indication of Phil's hidden misery, his yearning for the days that he had time off. This brings to mind the common phenomenon of spending working hours yearning for the weekend or the vacation.

Phil's occupation as a TV weatherman is not a source of any real satisfaction, the expression of any valued objective. The job is only a means to the end of occasional leisure and increased status. Leisure, at least for Phil, is a temporary "fix" that wears off the moment he is back on the job. And like David in *Lost In America*, the goal of increased status, once achieved, will prove to be an empty shadow, devoid of substance and meaning.

It is not that Phil's purpose has come into direct conflict with his TV station. Unlike Colonel Keith Davenport, who desires to preserve the lives of his men in in spite of General Prichard's unswerving dedication to using daylight precision bombing to help win the war, unlike Sonny Steele, who desperately seeks to preserve the soul of his cowboy self, unlike David, who recognizes that his cosmopolitan life style satisfies his inner needs, Phil has no purpose at all, no higher value that he seeks to satisfy. When he "punches" at life he is punching a bag of feathers. There is no pressure sent in return that can signal him to make adjustments that might be beneficial to his state of mind. He is not able to take care of his own soul.

A central theme of The Legend of the Dysfunctional System is that circumstance changes the near vacuum of a "bag of feathers" into pressure that can cause a person to move toward a solution to his problem. In Phil's case, the pressure to accomplish change, or at least achieve an attitude adjustment, may be there. Certainly the viewer can see the symptoms of hidden misery. But Phil does not perceive that he has a problem; everybody else does, but not Phil. He is living inside the trap of a reality that he has constructed for himself. What is the reality that Phil perceives? What is the cause of his hidden misery? How does this relate to his situation as a member of an organization?

Phil's behavior is antisocial: his deprecation of the innkeeper, his disdain for Ned, his arrogance toward his fellow workers and for the people of the town he is visiting. He is an individual who chooses not to act as a participant of a system. This describes his self-perception with respect to the human community in general and specifically to the organization of which he is a member. He perceives that there's nothing rewarding in accepting a role as a team player. His membership in the organization is valid in a formal sense, but does not affect his attitude or the way he behaves. He experiences the loneliness of the loner because he is interested only in individual outcomes, only what happens to him. He fails to see that by cooperating with others he might be more effective at his job and be more satisfied by his work. He fails to see that by interacting in a positive way with others he can be happier.

The words of Charles Dickens as he describes Scrooge might just as well have been said of Phil:

> Oh! But he was a tight-fisted hand at the grindstone, Scrooge! A squeezing, wrenching, grasping, clutching, covetous old

sinner! Hard and sharp as flint, from which no steel had ever struck out generous fire; secret, and self-contained, and solitary as an oyster. (Dickens 1984,10,11)

As Phil lives the same Groundhog Day over and over again he reveals to us that he wants very much to repudiate the rules made by others, the mandates of others, the specification of others for living a life that is good. Previously, he had to live by the rules of others or suffer the consequences. But the fantasy of the story places him in a situation where there is no tomorrow. Phil believes that only when tomorrow arrives does the rule-breaker suffers the consequences of his behavior. Accordingly, Phil has an opportunity to play out his most urgent fantasy, his most egotistical desire: the rejection, without risk to himself, of the guidelines that define civilization, the guidelines that prescribe a connection between individual human beings and social or organized systems.

Phil proclaims, "It is the same thing all your life...Be nice to your sister." He announces, "I am not going to live by their rules anymore." He meets Ned and punches him. This is assault. But by the next morning the assault did not happen. He eats unhealthy food. Why not? There are no consequences. He lets his cholesterol rise. He smokes. He proclaims, "I don't even have to floss." He drives wildly, defying the police and waking up the next morning, i.e. the same morning, without having to face the consequences of his defiance of the law. "I don't worry about anything anymore," he says. And this statement reveals what Phil's worry has been all along, reveals the source of his self-imposed isolation. Phil is afraid of losing control of his own life. He is afraid of living in a manner that is prescribed by others. Phil cannot be a member of a team because he rejects the rules that result in the cooperation of team members.

The story now gives Phil a way out of the trap of his own personal reality, a reality of the world as a demanding place where only an unsympathetic isolated person can survive and maintain his sanity. The ghosts of his past, present and future enabled Scrooge to escape from a life that was meaningless to himself. The unseen Fairy Godmother, or whatever supernatural being the viewer chooses to imagine, gives Phil the gift of freedom. This gift relieves him of the necessity to protect himself from the perceived harshness of mankind, gives him the capacity to experiment with his own life, starts him on the road from hidden misery to happiness.

The capacity of each person to take chances, to experiment with his life, and the desirability of doing so, weaves its way through the stories that comprise the Legend of the Dysfunctional System. Savage took a big chance when he held up the pilots' requests for transfer. Sonny took a big chance when he rode off with Rising Star. The calvarymen took a big chance when they fled with the doomed horses. David and Linda took a big chance when they went off to "touch an Indian." These chances are all part of a pattern of experimentation.

Like many of our mythical characters, Phil needs to break away from the reality, the rules, of others before he can find himself. In this way he can learn to accept responsibility for his own happiness, to gain control of his own life, to escape from having to defend himself from what he perceives is the nasty and brutish existence caused by "... their rules."

One February 2 turns into the next, and the next and the next...Phil's experiment places him on a power trip. He even dresses up as the hero in one of those Italian western movies, the Spaghetti Western, whose characters are even more macho and powerful than the ordinary cowboy hero portrayed in the American Westerns.

Now that Phil has established that he does not have to obey the rules of others, to fear the rules of others, he experiments by using the fantasy of his circumstances to control others. Nancy Taylor is a very pretty woman that Phil would like to know. The old antisocial Phil would have been inept at making contact. But the new Phil has a tool that the old Phil did not have: the capacity to obtain information about people and to use this to manipulate them. By coming into contact with Nancy each day and having a short conversation with her, he learns about her. He uses this information to cajole Nancy into believing that she knows him as a former but forgotten school mate. "I even asked you to the prom," he says. In this way Phil experiments with controlling the perceptions of others.

When he makes love to Nancy, he cries out to Rita, his producer. The intensity of sex has started to break the barrier between his surface self and his inner emotions. And his hidden emotions have a lot to do with Rita.

As he works his way through the phases of defiance and power, Phil's deep feelings for Rita emerge. His deeper self challenges his ego. The door that enables him to escape from his hidden misery is opening. He reaches out to Rita. He asks her, "If you only had one day to live, what would you do with it?"

Rita tells Phil what she wants: a man who is intelligent and supportive, kind, sensitive, gentle. She tells him that she likes animals, that she wants to change dirty diapers. Phil interacts with Rita the same way that he did with Nancy, by gathering information that he can use. He finds out what Rita's favorite drink is during a date on one day so he can order the same drink for himself during the same date replayed. He behaves like Rita's favorite man. Rita wants "world peace." He toasts "world peace." She is interested in 19th century French poetry. He recites some for her. Phil, of course, is faking it. He is interested neither in world peace nor in French poetry. Usually we think of "faking" as a negative behavior, dishonesty. But in the context of Phil's experiment, this is positive.

On the first day of many of my classes, I tell college students that a requirement of the course is that they be interested in the course material. I advise them that if they are not interested, they should fake interest. When they finish laughing or staring at me in amazement, I explain that sometimes faking it means giving something a chance in a way that you have not done before. Once you do this, I go on, maybe you will discover that you enjoy and are interested in the material after all.

Phil's imitation of Rita's favorite man has the impact on Phil I have suggested to my students. As he experiments, he starts genuinely to appreciate something new. For Phil, the something new is spontaneity. He is beginning a transformation. He will become someone like the Scrooge Dickens describes once the Spirits have shown him the causes of his own hidden misery.

"I don't know what day of the month it is!" said Scrooge. "I don't know how long I've been among the Spirits. I don't know anything. I'm quite a baby. Never mind. I don't care. I'd rather be a baby." (Dickens 1984, 128)

Phil joins Rita in a snowball fight with some local children. He dances with Rita and discovers the joy of the contact and the rhythm. Phil attacks the self-fulfilling prophesy that has pushed him into an unhappy existence. He has played the role of a mean and nasty person as a way of dealing with the conflict between his inner-self and his surface-self (ego). He acts negatively, but he also has the impulse to reach out and share his life with well-adjusted people like Rita. The two "parts" of Phil represent roles, the sets of values that are in conflict. We have already observed the discomfort of this condition in others, e.g. Sonny Steele in the conflicting roles of cowboy and salesman. One way of dealing with role conflict, of making all aspects of your feelings and behavior match up, as compared to being dissonant, is to act out one of the roles and reject the other. Sonny did this in his own way. He accepts the cowboy and rejects the salesman. Phil's way is to act out a self-fulfilling prophesy: to act out the role of the nasty person and bury the nice guy. He can't throw away the nice guy like Sonney threw away the salesman. The reward, for Phil, is the conclusion that he is at least living a consistent, albeit quietly desperate, life. This is the only way of coping with role conflict that Phil sees as workable.

Phil, however, learns that he has other choices. He can experiment with different roles. He can create different situations in the same way David and Linda played around with their lives. He tries something he was afraid to try before. At the end of a perfect day with Rita, Phil kisses her and tells her that he loves her. But somehow Rita realizes that she has been taken advantage of. "I can't believe I fell for this," she says. She leaves him.

Since the next day is the same day, he has a chance to have another perfect day with her. He tries the same day over and over again and at the end of each day she slaps his face. The song "But You Don't Know Me" playing on the sound track at this point gives us a hint concerning Rita's motivation for the continuing rejection of Phil.

Phil's first attempt at getting close to Rita has failed. He experiments with self-destructive behavior. He kidnaps the groundhog and drives off a cliff. No problem; the next day offers him another chance. He commits suicide by throwing a toaster into his bathtub. He jumps from a tower. He lives to experiment another day.

Phil is invulnerable. He says that he is "a god" and makes the comment that "... maybe the real God knows everything. Maybe he's just been around so long he knows everything." This is the insight that finally empowers Phil to escape from his hidden misery. Phil's experimentation is leading to a meritorious conclusion. He has discovered that knowledge, even wisdom, is the result of experience. Up to now, his experience has been limited by his own fear and lack of self-esteem. The plot of the fantasy has given him the chance to become a god...i.e. to become his authentic self. Rita is the catalyst for the emergence of Phil's godliness.

Phil complains to Rita that having to live the same day over and over is a curse. She tells him that maybe it is a blessing. The date that they have lived over and over again ends with her coming to his room in the Bed and Breakfast. She stays with him. But at 6 am it is the same day again and she is gone.

On the way to report on the continuing series of Groundhog Day ceremonies Phil gives money to a homeless beggar. He is friendly to all he meets. He pays $1000 for a piano lesson. Later he carves an ice sculpture. There is an artist in Phil and the artistic values are starting to emerge. He finds a role within himself that he had not previously imagined.

Because he is living the same day over and over, each piano lesson is his first. But because Phil carries the experience of each lesson into the next, i.e. the same, day he gets better and better. He uses the experience of the piano lesson to evoke the artist in him.

He meets Ned and gives him a big hug. Here is the role of "friend" emerging. An old homeless man dies. Phil looks at his chart in the hospital. He hopes to save him the next day. But the old man dies again despite Phil's attempt to save his life. Phil realizes that even with his seemingly magical powers he cannot control everything. There may be godliness in him, but he is not God.

Phil can, however, reap the benefits of his godliness, improve his self-esteem. There is a hero deep inside Phil. He needs to get others to recognize and to validate the hero. Only then can he recognize the hero in himself. He saves a boy who falls from a tree. He changes a flat tire for stranded ladies. He saves the Mayor from choking to death by administering first aid. He uses his newly acquired musical skills to dazzle the celebrants at the Groundhog Day party.

At the party, the ladies of the town bid in an auction for the company of bachelors. The proceeds will go to charity. Rita, having observed Phil's good deeds, realizes she is in love with him. She bids $339.88, all she has, and wins his company.

Phil carves an ice statue in Rita's image. Phil says that no matter what happens tomorrow, he is happy. This is a new form of self-fulfilling prophesy, one much better calculated to help Phil achieve happiness.

He awakens. It is 6AM, but this time Rita is still next to him. He proclaims, "Something is different." Indeed that is true. This is the next day. The ground is covered with snow. It is tomorrow. Phil says "Let's live here." The story ends to the refrain of the song "It's Almost Like Being in Love."

At first glance, the film Groundhog Day is a lighthearted comedy. But as we have seen, much in the way of useful analysis can be gleaned from taking a closer look at Phil, who is forced by a fantastic set of circumstances more closely to examine himself and his relationship with social and organizational systems.

As a teacher, I can certainly relate to living the same semester, if not the same day, over and over. Burnout can be a professional hazard of teaching, just as Phil was burned out by his yearly visits to the Punxsatawney. Each academic year I am a year older, yet the students' faces seem to remain the same. I set up shop in the same classrooms, deal with the same problems, repeat the same processes.

This repetition, as it was for Phil, can be a source of enlightenment and pleasure. But this happens only when I pay careful attention. Each semester is the same. Each semester is different. If I can recognize the differences in my behavior and the way I am either more effective or less effective, if I can recognize the way that changes in my behavior affect my own satisfaction and reduce the gap between the purpose of myself, that of my students and that of my school, I can come one step closer to my inner-self and to the sort of joy that Phil finally discovers.

Phil found out that life can be a grand experiment, where knowledge and wisdom can be harvested as the result of experience, even repeated experience. Perhaps Phil hit the nail right on the head when he speculated that God knows everything because he has been around so long.

Chapter Seven

The Problem of Location-Hierarchy: The Cases of *Twelve O'clock High, Patton, The Caine Mutiny, Catch 22*

Definition of Politics: A process that determines who gets what, when, and how.   Harold D.Laswell

There is an "iron law" of real estate. It asserts that the three factors which determine the value of property are: location, location, and location. A person's location in an organization is similarly important. It determines the extent that his values can conflict with those of his organization. It determines the nature and intensity of the conflict between individual and organizational purpose.

Where you are located in the organization is determined by seniority and specialization. Both of these characteristics are displayed on the ubiquitous organization chart, the wiring diagram of the organization that displays the vertical and horizontal dimensions of the organization.

This chart, supplemented by the formal job descriptions published in organization manuals and in contracts, constitutes the design of the organization.The design shows the way that the labor of the organization is divided: vertically, with respect to each person's position in the hierarchy and, horizontally, with respect to the specialized functions that are to be performed by each person.

Let's look at the way the phenomenon of location shows up as a key element in the situation of organizational participants. The bureaucratic design exists to satisfy the increasing requirement for knowledge and skill brought about by the industrial revolution and intensified during the postindustrial era. The seminal assumptions of bureaucracy are:

(1) The person at the top of a hierarchy knows the best way to get things done.

and

(2) The requirement for expertise must be fragmented because no one person or group of people can possess all the knowledge or skills necessary to get things done.

General Prichard, in *Twelve O'clock High*, sits at the very top of the hierarchy of the U.S. Army Air Corps forces in England. His position in the organization is based on the assumption that he has more knowledge than anyone else in the organization concerning the best way that these forces can contribute to winning the war. He is the source of strategic decisions, the master of the big picture. He is the highest authority, the "author" of the "story" that is played out by bomber operations.

General Savage sits just below Prichard as Commander of the 918th Bomber Group. His position is based on the assumption that he has more knowledge than anybody else in the 918th concerning the coordination of the efforts of the members of the group, more skill at prescribing the best tactics to implement Pritchard's strategic decisions.

The vertical dimension of the organization's ladder descends in this manner all the way down to the Group Clerk, Ernie. Ernie's rank fluctuates back and forth from Sergeant to Private depending on the extent that Savage honors assumptions concerning Ernie's capacity to exercise authority at the lower levels of the organization.

The Problem of Location-Hierarchy

The horizontal division of labor in the 918th is described by the arrangements for the use of those distinct and diverse skills necessary to accomplish the mission.

The organization chart displays: the Ground Executive Officer, Major Harvey Stoval, an expert at administration; the Air Executive Officer, Major Joe Cob, an expert at the conduct of air operations; the Group Flight Surgeon, Doc Kaiser, an expert at the physiology and psychology of flight crews; the Chaplain, who in the words of General Savage confines his expertise to "the area of sin" and the pilots, navigators and gunners whose distinct skills contribute to the capacity of each aircraft to put bombs on enemy targets.

The problems faced by individuals are often caused by their location on the hierarchical ladder of the organization. Ernie's self-esteem is dependent on the way General Savage chooses to exercise his authority. Because Savage is a stickler for the formal regulations, every time Ernie violates these, no matter how insignificant the violation, Ernie has to remove his Sergeant stripes. Because Savage values loyalty and devotion to the mission, Ernie gets to sew the stripes back on when Savage learns he has stowed away on a bomber to perform duties as a gunner. Savage's authority is the cause of Ernie's problem as well as the source of Ernie's satisfaction.

Sometimes Savage is a source of comfort for Ernie, sometimes a source of pain. In any event, the Golden Rule of Hierarchy is, "He who has the gold, makes the rule!"

The horizontal division of labor, the specialization of function, at times cause problems for the individual. Doc Kaiser perceives air operations through the lens of his expertise. He knows that the men can only take so much, that they are not machines. He looks at the evidence that the sick list is getting longer, that the incidence of psychosomatic complaints is becoming more frequent. He concludes that the level of stress is too high.

Doc knows that the men are supposed to put out a maximum effort. But he is troubled because nobody has defined maximum effort in terms that are consistent with his expertise, i.e. in medical terms. Doc's perspective is a result of Doc's job description. And this perspective is in conflict with Savages' perspective. Savage is concerned with the necessity to keep flying regardless of the consequences to the physical and emotional condition of the crews. The Air Executive Officer does not cancel flights because the crews' reserves of physical and emotional strength have been exhausted.

The crews themselves are in conflict with the perspective of Doc Kaiser. They have decided to risk their lives, to sacrifice their lives in the name of the mission. Indeed, the way the entire chain-of-command perceives the situation is in conflict with Doc's professional values.

The division of labor vertically and horizontally is the response of the modern organization to the complexity of modern life. At the same time that it helps deal with complexity, however, the division of labor creates two distinct fundamental problems.

I will discuss the first of these, hierarchy, in this chapter. In the following chapter I will discuss the problem of specialization.

The top of the hierarchical ladder is usually occupied by fewer people than the middle. The middle is more sparsely populated than the bottom. The utility of bureaucracy is that it gives to the few the possibility of controlling the many. That is why we represent the shape of the organization as narrow at the top and wide at the bottom, a triangle.

In theory, the capability of a leader to blend the various perspectives of people at differing rungs on the ladder of hierarchy and in different areas of specialization resolves the problem of location. In theory, the person in a position of high authority not only is best prepared with knowledge concerning the tasks at hand, he is also best prepared to use human resources in an effective way, a way that optimizes the human contribution to the organizational enterprise and that minimizes the conflict between organizational and individual purpose.

Yet the Legend Of The Dysfunctional System tells us that sometimes there is a wide gap between theory and practice, tells us that the capacity of leaders to effect harmony of

The Problem of Location-Hierarchy

purpose is neither a universal nor even a common condition. The reasons for this are both idiosyncratic, having to do with the characteristics of a particular leader, and systemic, having to do with the very nature of modern organizations.

Let's focus on a leader who is positioned at the apex of the bureaucratic triangle but who does not posses the skills and knowledge assumed by the bureaucratic model.

The film *The Caine Mutiny* gives us a look at the archetypical ineffective leader, a look at the problem of location that is caused by the bureaucratic phenomenon of hierarchy.

In *The Caine Mutiny*, Captain Queeg leads the motley crew of a motley ship. He exhibits behavior that is considered to be bizarre and even psychotic by his officers, especially by Lieutenant Keefer. Keefer is a novelist in civilian life. He is writing a book that will tell the tale of the ship.

Captain Queeg has many weaknesses. He is a coward who turns his ship to retreat in the face of enemy fire. He is an incompetent seaman who circles his ship aimlessly until it cuts the rope that is used to tow a target for other ships to practice gunnery. He is a martinet who mobilizes the crew into a criminal investigation when some strawberries are missing from the galley larder. The climax of the story captures the portrait of an incompetent leader.

The U.S.S Caine is cruising in formation with a large task force bound for an important engagement with the enemy. To stay in the formation the ship must maintain the course and speed that is common to all ships in the group. When a typhoon engulfs the Caine, a decision crisis is presented to the officers on the bridge: Queeg, Lieutenant Steve Maryk, who is Queeg's second in command, and the more junior Willie Keith.

The wind and sea are coming from aft of the ship. In these conditions control of the ship is very difficult. There is a distinct danger that the ship will founder, become uncontrollable, capsize and sink as it falls victim to the forces of nature pushing it sideways.

Queeg insists on holding the task force's prescribed course and speed. Those are his orders, orders designed to achieve the formal mission of the ship: accompany other ships in the task force to the area of intended engagement with the enemy.

Queeg has lost communication with the task force commander so he must make his own decision based on his own perception of the facts and his own values. He elects to maintain course and speed because he values the Caine's formal mission and because he values his own career. He fears that breaking from the formation will result in incurring the wrath of his superiors.

As the Captain of the ship (positioned at the apex of the ladder of authority) Queeg's judgment should remain unimpaired in stressful situations. Yet in the story of the Caine, the assumption of leader competence in stressful situations is not valid.

Steve Maryk, second in command, is an excellent and experienced seaman. He fears the loss of the ship and its crewmen, including himself. Maryk cannot be certain that the ship will be lost if the Caine not slowed and turned about into the face of oncoming wind and sea. But Maryk's value premise places the lives of the crew and the survival of the ship over the continued blind pursuit of the mission.

Maryk, supported by his fellow officer Willie Keith, relieves Captain Queeg of all duties. He justifies this action with the proclamation that the Captain is ill and cannot continue in command. Queeg gives up his command without a fight. Maryk is now in charge. He turns the ship into the wind. The ship is saved. The audience heaves a great sigh of relief!

We often think of weak leadership as the source of problems for followers. We believe that the cause of weak leadership is the placement of an ill-behaved or corrupt person in a position of high authority.

The story of the Caine Mutiny, however, tells us that this is not necessarily so. The story tells us that the problem of hierarchy is not fully explained by the personal characteristics of the leader, that the seeds of disharmony and individual pain can be found in the very soil, in the founding assumptions, of bureaucracy itself.

The Problem of Location-Hierarchy 77

The story does not imply that Queeg is a bad person. The effectiveness of the organizational structure depends on the competence of authority, not necessarily on the virtue of authority. The story even goes as far as to suggest that Queeg is indeed a virtuous person, that Queeg is the good guy and Maryk the bad guy.

Steve Maryk is put on trial. A naval court martial will determine whether or not he is guilty of mutiny. Maryk is defended by a brilliant lawyer-naval officer, Barney Greenwald.

Greenwald's brutal examination of Queeg on the stand results in the emotional breakdown of the Caine's captain. Queeg is a broken man. The officers of the court martial conclude that Queeg is indeed sick and they exonerate Maryk.

Once again the audience, which has been rooting for Maryk and hooting Queeg, heaves a sigh of relief.

But there is more. At the party to celebrate the victory of those who brought down Captain Queeg, Barney Greenwald enters. He is drunk. He is congratulated by the officers of the Caine and asked to join them in celebration. But he refuses to do so. The reasons for his refusal shed light on the distinction between virtue and competence in a leader.

Lawyer Barney Greenwald tells the assembled jubilant officers that defending Maryk was his job and he did the best he could. But to successfully defend the accused mutineer, Barney had to destroy Queeg. And Barney feels very badly about this. "When Hitler was preparing to turn my grandmother into soap," asks Barney, "where was Willie Keith? Where was Keefer?"

Barney goes on to point out that that the former was having fun as a student at Princeton and the latter was writing his novels. And where was Queeg? He was, as a career naval officer, on duty ready to defend the downtrodden of the world from evil, ready to protect democracy, ready to protect Barney Greenwald's grandmother.

Notwithstanding Queeg's individual weaknesses, explains the lawyer, the organization to which he devoted his life was useful and good, more useful and good than the junior officers of the Caine, the civilian-sailors that had brought Queeg down and brought discredit upon the organization.

Some people are thrust into positions of leadership and are just not capable of dealing with the problems that leaders face.

The fact that this is not an uncommon occurrence is explained, at least in part, by the "Peter Principle": People rise in organizations until they reach a level at which they are incompetent. Where and when a leader falls victim to the "Peter Principle" depends on the competence of the particular individual and the difficulty of the particular situation.

Captain Queeg may have been capable of handling his duties in peacetime. He is even admired by the Navy lawyer Greenwald for spending a lifetime in the professional military to be ready to fight when war comes. But when war does come and Queeg is put in charge of the U.S.S. Caine, his leadership ability falls far short of what is required.

The bureaucratic assumptions concerning the knowledge and skill of leaders in positions of authority may be valid in some circumstances and not in others. It is the latter contingency that causes problems for organizational participants.

We have seen that one flaw of bureaucratic structure is discovered by examining the generic situation of the leader, the variation between his required competence and his actual competence. We have seen that the assumption of leader competence is tested in the context of particular situations.

Furthermore, the Legend Of The Dysfunctional System tells us of another problem generated by the variation between the real and the ideal leader. In the ideal, a leader is the personification of his organization. His purpose and the mission of the organization are coincidental, his goals and the goals of the organization are the same. Bureaucracy assumes that a leader will overcome his human weakness and become the unselfish director of the organization's story.

The bureaucratic structure not only assumes leadership competence, it assumes leadership selflessness. In reality, however, the leader may use the organization and its members to satisfy his own needs. The leader may behave in a

The Problem of Location-Hierarchy

way that displaces the goals of the organization and the goals of those people who inhabit it.

Leaders as well as followers are players in the game of organizational life. The indicator of their effectiveness as players is the survival and success of their organizations. But leaders are human beings.

We should not perceive the role of leader to be only that of an abstract personification of the organization. The individual values and needs (i.e. the purpose) of the leader, just as is the case with any other human participant, can be in conflict with the mission or even the survival of the organization, and in conflict with the well being of the organization's people. This is the paradox of leadership. A number of the stories that comprise The Legend of the Dysfunctional System make this point.

In the film *Network*, the top executives decide to murder a neurotic news hour anchorman, Howard, when he becomes a threat to their positions of power. We may reasonably predict that such a decision will come back to haunt the organization, to cause the organization to pay a great price. In any event, Howard loses his life because his leaders were willing to sacrifice him, and in the longer run the organization, for their own selfish ends.

In the film *Patton*, the famous General makes decisions that optimize his own personal power and glory rather than the probability of strategic success.

General Patton races the British, under the command of General Montgomery, to Palermo, the end point of the alliance drive in Sicily, not because that is the optimal way of accomplishing the organization's objective, but because Patton wants the glory of getting to Palermo first, the glory of liberating the citizens of Palermo.

And General Patton does this at the cost of the brave American soldiers who die in pursuit of his personal goal, soldiers he admires very much. One can only wonder whether General Patton's admiration of bravery among his subordinates is motivated by their contribution to the mission of the organization or by their contribution to his own personal glory.

In the film *Catch 22*, Colonel Cathcart orders his pilots to fly in very tight formations, even though that is a demanding and dangerous tactic. Cathcart wants to achieve a good clean aerial photograph, one that he won't be ashamed to send through channels.

General Peckem recommends that the men wear full dress uniforms on combat missions so they'll make a good impression on the enemy when they are shot down.

The men are promised by their leaders that they will be rotated out of combat after flying 25 missions. But Colonel Cathcart determines that his unit should average more combat missions per person that any other unit. Accordingly, he continues to raise the number of combat missions required. This increase in appaarent unit accomplishment will increase the Colonel's chances for promotion.The goal of pilotmorale and the goal of pilot survival has been displaced by the goal of Cathcart's promotion.

It is only by feigning insanity that the flyers can escape their combat duties. The rules require Colonel Cathcart to ground any flyer who is mentally unfit to fly. Colonel Cathcart requires a flyer who desires to be excused from combat to justify his request on the grounds of his own insanity.

But there is a catch: Catch 22. If a man asks to be excused from combat by reason of his own insanity, that constitutes prima facie evidence that he comprehends the perils of combat, that he has a rational mind, that he is indeed sane.

The rationality of some of the pilots results in the confession that they are insane. The rationality of Colonel Cathcart results in the declaration that a confession of insanity is proof of sanity.

Catch-22 seems to be a rule that thwarts the survival needs of the pilots. From the perspective of flyers like Yosarrian, it certainly is. But from the perspective of people like Colonel Cathcart, Catch-22 is eminently functional. It keeps pilots on the job despite combat fatigue. It optimizes the number of missions per pilot. It creates the illusion of leadership effectiveness. It increases the chance that Colonel Cathcart will one day be General Cathcart.

As the world of ideas focuses on the politics of organizational life, there are very few notions that are considered to state unconditional truths, very few propositions that are considered to be "laws" (like the law of gravity in physics).

An exception is the Iron Law of Oligarchy. (Michels 1949) This law states that in organized groups of people the many will always be lead by the few. A corollary of this law suggested by The Legend Of The Dysfunctional System is that the few will always have the opportunity to use the many for their own selfish purpose.

James Madison makes the point in the *Federalist Papers* that "...men are not angels." He goes on to point out that if men were angels there would be no need for government. Madison's solution to the problem that men are not angels was to design a government where men would share power, a government where the power of some would serve as a check on the power of others.

Similarly, the leaders of organizations are not angels. They are neither absolutely virtuous nor absolutely knowledgeable. If they were, they could design a perfect organization and merely push a button and let it run.

If leaders were absolutely knowledgeable, there would be no need for them to share the decision making process with subordinates, there would be no need for expertise or judgment at lower levels of the organization.

However, in many, organizations the complex nature of the organization's tasks and environment requires that power not only be derived from elevated position, but that it also be granted to those with specialized expertise.

The characteristic of specialized expertise is designed into the organization to act as a check on the power of those at the top of the hierarchy. But this can compound the problems of individuals as they swim in the organizational sea.

In the next chapter we will look at what the Legend of the Dysfunctional System has to say about the problem of specialization.

Chapter Eight

The Problem of Location-Specialization : The Case of *Executive Suite*

"Where you stand is determined by where you sit."
The Essence of Decision, Graham Allison

The anatomy of modern organizations concentrates authority at the top. Yet in many organizations the complex nature of tasks requires that power not only be derived from elevated position, but that it also be granted to those with specialized expertise. The "Generals" of organizations are generalists who are not necessarily knowledgeable concerning the technical details of all tasks that must be performed. Specialized experts, professionals, are used to advise the generalist-leader, to perform specialized tasks and, when necessary, are given some amount of discretionary authority. After all, the boss is not always there to make a decision. And if he were, he might mess things up.

Specialized expertise acts as a check and a balance on the power of those at the top of the hierarchy. But this can compound the problems of the lower level specialist as his purpose comes into conflict with the purpose of other individuals and with that of the organizational system. In this chapter we will look at what the Legend of the Dysfunctional System has to say about the problem of specialization.

The film *Executive Suite* tells the story of a struggle for power at the very top of a corporation. But this story is more than a struggle among people for personal dominance. The plot reveals a clash of values. Each actor in the drama is the personification of values that are the result of a perspective formed by the person's specialized function and expertise. The mind set of each individual is formed by the particular contribution that each makes to the organized system. What each person does (his area of specialization) determines what each person is (his values). And what each person is determines his point of view concerning the organization's strategy and decisions. Since the labor is divided among those who perform specialized functions, there is bound to be conflict among the players, conflict that is present irrespective of each player's desire for personal power, per se.

The engineer in a firm that manufactures automobiles wants to build a car that is efficient and reliable. That's what engineers do. The marketing manager wants to build a car that looks good to the buying public and will therefore be fashionable and popular, i.e. will sell. That's what marketing people do. The engineer and the marketeer may not be involved in a power struggle. They may be best friends who wish each other the utmost of happiness. Yet, when a tradeoff must be made between running well and looking good, there will be (inherent) conflict between the two.

Those who come out on top of the race for organizational reward, those who rise from specialist to generalist, will carry their perspective with them. If the accountant rises to the top, his leadership will be saturated with the criteria of financial management. If the engineer rises to the top, the firm will more than likely be infused with the norm of quality of product.

At the top of the organization described in the film *Executive Suite* is Avery Bulloch, the President of Treadway

Corporation. The firm manufactures furniture. Bulloch became president when the company founder died. Bulloch is an effective leader who has brought Treadway from a small company that produced luxury furniture to a very profitable firm with a wide range of products designed for a mass market. Profits, value of stock, and stockholder dividends have all risen dramatically under the command of Bulloch. Bulloch's role has been one of savior. He rescued the company which, upon the death of its founder, was likely to become a ship without a rudder. But he has unwittingly subverted the vision of the founder: to focus on quality of product, to value pride over profit, to focus on the market niche that stresses quality.

The leadership structure, the people that inhabit the Executive Suite at the very top of the headquarters building, consists of a group of Vice Presidents all of whom report directly to Avery Bulloch, all of whom are located on the same horizontal element of the firm's wiring diagram. There is no Executive Vice President. This scheme has worked because Treadway has been a one man corporation, dominated by the charismatic and brilliant Bulloch. The hierarchical levels below the President have not acted to check and balance power so as to infuse the vision of the leader with fresh ideas and different perspectives. Bulloch is driven by a personal crusade to maintain the viability and strength of the firm. He is, moreover, romantically involved with Julia Treadway, the daughter of the firm's founder. Julia became a major stockholder when her father died. Her problem is that Avery Bulloch loves the firm more than he loves her.

Bulloch has called a meeting of the firm's Executive Committee, a governing body that represents both the stockholders and management. The Committee consists of Bulloch who is President and Chairman of the Board, five Vice Presidents (all of whom are also Directors with membership on the Board), Julia Treadway, as a major stock holder and Director, and George Caswell, a Director. Everyone assumes that Bulloch has called the meeting for the purpose of designating an Executive Vice President and successor. Apparently, Bulloch's authoritarian stewardship of Treadway is no longer necessary.

On the way to the meeting of the Executive Committee, Avery Bulloch drops dead of a heart attack. The inhabitants of the Executive Suite now have to determine who will be the next President. The struggle for power has begun. The future strategy of the corporation, the essence of its evolving mission, the culture of the organization, what the organization becomes, will be determined by those values that dominate the persona of the winner. Up to now the culture, the shared values and beliefs of the corporate executives, has been represented by the beliefs and values of Bulloch. With his death, this culture evaporates. The only common characteristic among executives has been a respect for Bulloch. Now that he is gone, each player will shed the mask of the Bulloch-driven culture and don the mask of his own individuality. Now that Bulloch is gone, the centrifugal forces that existed all along can come into play.

George Caswell is interested only in personal wealth and a lavish life style. The firm is his cash cow. He lives off the dividends of his stock holdings and by his market-savey wits. He is the first to learn of Bulloch's death. He tries to take advantage of the situation by selling company stock short in a shady deal that will make him rich when the stock value drops as the public learns of Bulloch's death. Caswell, since he has no expertise relevant to the running of the firm, is not at all a candidate for managerial power.

Jim Anderson is the company Treasurer. He is a contemporary of Bulloch and has been his closest confidant in the firm. Anderson has stood by Bulloch's side as he saved Treadaway. Had Bulloch lived, Anderson would probably have been his successor. His ties to Bulloch, ironically, are now his weakness. His vision for Treadway is very similar to those of the founder of the firm: dominating the niche for luxury furniture, deriving more satisfaction from pride in product than from profits. Most of the players believe that this vision is outdated and that the firm needs to grow and increase profit, and increase the return on investment for the stockholders.

The Problem of Location-Specialization

The specialized function performed by Anderson has been to be the guardian of the old culture and a shadow President to Bulloch. For Anderson, the purpose of Treadway is to reflect the personality of its leader, to preserve the image and memory of its founder and of Anderson's best friend, the late Bulloch. Anderson will not change. Because of this and because of his age, Anderson is more a King Maker than a potential King.

Other Vice President's have their own agendas. These are derived from where they sit in the organization. Instead of having an outlook that can optimize the accomplishments of the organization, each will suboptimize, i.e. work to achieve those results that are important to their own particular compartmentalized parts of the organization.

Jessie Grim is Vice President for manufacturing operations. As long as the factories are running well, he is satisfied. He has neither the appetite nor the vision to steer Treadway into the future. His horizons are limited by the details of the manufacturing process. He is not a suitable President.

Walt Dudley is Vice President for Sales. He is the quintessential salesman. His strength is that he is popular among the customers of the firm. Like many other expert salesmen, what he has been selling for years is himself. Whatever the strategy of the company, Walt is willing and able to sell product, any product. Because of this he is a great asset. But popularity is not what is needed to lead this organization. Walt has neither the inclination nor the skills to stand at the apex of the hierarchy.

This leaves the two main contenders: Loren Shaw, Comptroller, and Don Walling, Vice President for Design. The opposing mind sets of these two form the drama of the battle for the soul of the Treadway Corporation.

Loren Shaw is Treadway's Comptroller. He wants the job of President badly. He is a numbers man. He does accounting; he is an accountant. As a leader, he will hold his followers accountable for the numbers that they generate (sales, costs, profits, price of stock etc.). Shaw sees organizational life exclusively in terms of the quantitative goals of the firm. His persona is as cold and hard as the statistics that are his focus.

Nobody likes him. Typical of Shaw's behavior is his resistance to the idea of closing factories on the day of Bulloch's funeral. He calculates that the cost of such a "paid vacation" would be $87,000.

Caswell needs Shaw if he is to pull off the shady stock deal. The others need him because he is perceived, as a hardheaded realistic businessman, to be most capable of ensuring the continued viability of the firm. The most significant indicator of success for Shaw is return on investment for stockholders. Indeed, for him this is the sole purpose of Treadway. This is what Shaw means when he says, " I only have one interest, the good of the firm." This is a short term perspective because stockholders want to draw on high dividends and to be able to sell their stock at a profit. For them, the vision of the founder has nothing to do with the purpose of the organization.

Don Walling is Vice President for Design. He is an engineer. His function is to develop product and manufacturing processes that will meet the highest standards of function and beauty and will take advantage of state-of-the-art techniques. His latest passion is the development of a new molding process that will improve the quality of the furniture produced by Treadway. The power struggle that occurs upon the death of Bulloch is more an annoying distraction for Walling than an opportunity. He has a great need for engineering achievement and not much of a desire for personal power. He would rather keep working on his new designs than attend the Board meetings that will determine the fate of the firm.

Walling is a man who has great pride in the product he designs. He has great empathy for the plant workers. Most of these people are long time employees who started working for Treadway in the days of the corporation's founder. Their psychic income of pride in product is threatened by what they see as the wave of the future. They fear becoming mere pawns in the corporate profit seeking numbers game. Walling, as he considers the future of the firm under Shaw, has the same fear. The workers consider themselves to be craftsmen rather than employees. Walling considers himself to be an engineer rather than a profit maximizing manager.

The Problem of Location-Specialization

Of course, individual desire for power is an important factor in this situation. Walling is not so much an idealist that he fails to understand the impact of individual power on the future of the firm.

But the struggle for victory is not the only important motivation for the contenders. Shaw wants power. But he also wants the firm to conform to the standards, procedures and values of his function in the organization: accounting.

Walling has very little taste for power, per se. But he wants the firm to conform to the standards and aspirations of his function in the organization: his role as design engineer. His fear of losing control of his capacity to conform to engineering values convinces him to throw his hat into the ring, to challenge Loren Shaw in the competition for President.

Julia Treadway is the key to what happens next. She holds the crucial vote. But she is devastated by the death of Bulloch and has no taste for the game. She gives her proxy to Shaw and for a while it seems as though Shaw will be the next President. The prospect of Shaw as President shocks Walling out of his complacency.

In a climactic scene Walling prevents the despondent Julia from leaping out of the Executive Suite window. He convinces her that she can, by voting for him, preserve the vision of her father and atone for the way that her lover perverted this vision. She withdraws her proxy from Shaw and casts the pivotal vote that enthrones Walling. In the end, what she has done is determined by who she is: her father's daughter.

It is in this way that the ethic of product quality is passed from one generation to the next. But the rebirth of the organization takes place in an environment of and pain and disharmony.

The role that each expert accepts is determined by the values derived from the nature of his particular expertise. Organizational leaders demand socialization that involves acceptance of the purpose of mission. But the development of expertise demands socialization that involves acceptance of values determined by the specialized function. This places individuals in conflict with the organized system and with each other.

In the next chapter we will explore the problem of professionalism, a particular form of specialization, by unpacking the idea of role a even more exhaustively.

Chapter Nine

The Problem of Professionalism: The Cases of *The Right Stuff, A Few Good Men*

"No Buck Rogers, no bucks!" *The Right Stuff*, Tom Wolfe

In Chapter Five we explored the notion of role conflict. Here the problem for the individual was that he found himself in a situation where there was a need to conform to two contradictory roles (sets of values) at the same time. Sonny Steele (in *Electric Horseman*), for example, found that his cowboy set of values were in conflict with what was expected of him as a corporate symbol. David (in *Lost In America*) similarly experienced the inner conflict between his role as a corporate executive and his desire to conform to the ideals that motivated him upon graduation from college. Role conflict in these cases involves the pulls and hauls that exist within the psyche of the individual. Here, roles compete for the possession of person.

There is another problem that can be understood in terms of the concept of role. This problem concerns the conflict between different people who assume contradictory roles.

When an organization formulates job descriptions, it creates a mold (role) that it expects, indeed needs, individuals to play. Thus we see Shaw as the accountant and Walling as the engineer because Treadway Corporation needs an accountant and also needs an engineer. The two men succeed in their jobs because they accept their assigned roles. And as they do so, the conflict between the two is predictable.

The inner conflict that individuals experience that we have called role conflict is resolved when the individual unambiguously chooses one preferred role. David, in *Lost In America*, rejected the role of freewheeling gypsy and accepted the role of corporate midlevel executive because he needed to resolve his inner conflict. The firm provided him a way out of his dilemma. Savage, in *Twelve O'clock High*, does the same thing when he attempts to assume the singular role of General by rejecting the father role. Davenport, on the other hand, lets down the organization when he rejects the role of Colonel to be comfortable with his persona of fatherly protector of comrades.

The focus on one role, one area of specialization, can become a form of coping with the emotional stress of role conflict. As an individual becomes increasingly focused on a singular set of values derived from a particular expertise, he becomes a professional: an expert who shares values with others who apply the same expertise and who sees his function as having a responsibility to society that transcends his responsibility to an employer. (Huntington 1957)

The process of professionalization is one of continual development of particular skills and continual socialization into particular sets of values. As this happens, the professional is likely to experience conflict of a sort that is distinct from the inner stress of role conflict, as in *Twelve O'clock High*, and from the conflict among individuals that has its source in assignment to perform a specialized function for an organization, as in *Executive Suite*.

In the abstract, professional expertise and values can be the basis of a well integrated persona for the individual and the foundation for harmony among colleagues. But this very inner peace and harmony among professional colleagues can become an (ironic) source of conflict. First of all, professionals inevitably come into conflict with managers. Secondly, professionals can come into conflict with society in general. Let's start by exploring the nearly ubiquitous conflict that exists between professionals and their managers.

The film *The Right Stuff* chronicles the adventures of the original seven Project Mercury astronauts, the first Americans in space. Because the job description "astronaut" had not previously existed, these seven men were chosen from the occupation that seemed most closely to resemble the emerging profession of astronaut. They were all military test pilots.

As test pilots, the seven men shared the expertise of flying experimental aircraft to the limits of designed performance envelopes and beyond. They shared the ego satisfaction of the daredevil. They shared the discretionary power granted to them by military organizations that were dependent upon them to maintain United States dominance in military aviation. They shared the isolation from management provided by the secrecy of their tasks, the esoteric nature of their duties, the high risks inherent to their mission, and the unpredictability of their airborne experimentation.

The movie introduces us to the test pilot as a free spirit. This role is personified by the quintessential of all test pilots, Chuck Yeager. When we look at his life style, we see a picture of a man that is much more in touch with himself and his compatriots than with his bureaucratic organization, the Air Force.

As military test pilots, these men were not at all in conflict with their organization. In fact, they were isolated from the organization, practicing as individual artists responding to the whim of the soul rather than to the dictates of managers, dictates like the necessity to use only standard operating procedures. Savage and the 918th Bomber Group, in *Twelve O'clock High*, may have been flying in accordance with the orders of General Pritchard. But these test pilots were flying by the seat of their *own* pants.

The competition for assignment to the civilian agency, NASA, and for the designation astronaut is intense. Only those who have the right stuff will be selected. But what, exactly, is the right stuff? And how, if at all, does it differ from the stuff that it takes to be a test pilot?

The seven men who are selected believe that the transition from military test pilot to astronaut involves only an upgrade in status. They seek this recognition and see their new profession as no different from the old one. Significantly, Chuck Yeager chooses not to compete for the astronaut job, but rather to remain in his military test pilot job. Yeager realizes that the transition to astronaut will involve more than just a change in uniform and title.

As newly minted astronauts, the seven men become part of a highly politicized, highly bureaucratized agency, NASA. The U.S. is losing a race with the Soviets who have already placed an orbiting manned satellite into space. The technology is speculative. Development of the project is in the hands of NASA bureaucrat-managers and rocket scientists imported from post-World War II Germany. The politics of the process are driven by the President's promise to put an American on the Moon within ten years.

NASA integrates the astronauts into the agency, not as independent practitioners of an esoteric and heroic art, but as tools in a complex organizational machine designed to accomplish the man-in-space mission quickly and efficiently. The problem for the astronauts is that the act of probing space, per se, and the act of placing a man in space are not at all the same thing. In fact, placing a man in a space capsule complicates the task of placing the capsule in space.

There is no doubt that the technology exists to navigate in space by remote control. The human need not be in the cockpit to control the craft. Indeed the earliest space probes were manned by a chimpanzee. And if there is human presence, the requirement for life support systems and the use of over-engineering to provide for safety grossly complicates the technical problem of space exploration. From the perspective of the scientists designing the Mercury spacecraft, and from the perspective of those managing the project, the man is redundant, if not useless, an obstacle to success. Because of this Chuck Yeager has referred to the astronaut not as a brave and skillful pilot controlling the course and the fate of his craft and himself, but as "Spam in the can!"

As the training of the seven astronauts nears an end and as the Mercury capsule nears the completion of its construction, the seven men are shocked to see that the prototype capsule has no window. From an engineering perspective the addition of a window would weaken the structural integrity of the craft. Moreover, managers are keeping their eye on the prize of efficiency. From the managerial perspective, the window is an unnecessary cost that produces no useful effect. Yeager, it seems, was right. The seven men realize that they are going to be "Spam in the can" after all, just along for the ride.

The unhappy professional-astronaut-specialist now has come into severe conflict with his organization. Six of the seven have no idea how to deal with this conflict. The seventh, John Glenn, has the right stuff in a way that was not anticipated by the test pilots turned astronaut, by NASA, or by those who selected these men for the job. Glenn believes that a man in the capsule is necessary because only the presence of the human expert will be able to deal with all the contingencies that space exploration will involve. But this is a matter of faith rather than demonstrable fact.

The right stuff that Glenn is made of is the stuff of organizational politics. He realizes that the prize of space exploration and dominance may be achieved without the assistance of an on-board pilot. But he also realizes that support for the expensive project depends on public opinion and its impact on the government in general and on Congress in particular. Public support, Glenn realizes, depends on the heroic image of the astronaut rather than on engineering efficiency or managerial cost-effectiveness criteria.

Glenn takes charge of the situation and solves his colleagues' problem by informing NASA scientists, engineers, and administrators that without a window the seven will withdraw from the project. If this happens, he informs his seniors, there is no pilot for the craft and without a pilot there are no heroes. And without heroes there will be no public support. "No Buck Rogers," Glenn tells them, "no bucks."

The managers of the project realize that Glenn is right, that Glenn has more power that would be revealed by the organizational chart. They order the construction of a window.

In this movie we see the juxtaposition of the role of the professional and the manager. The result is the emergence of organizational politics. We see the battle between those who see the practice of their profession as a happiness producing end in itself (in this case the test pilots) and those who see expertise as a cost effective contribution to some systemic effect expressed in terms of an organizational mission (in this case the NASA managers).

The emergence of this sort of conflict is inevitable because at the core of the manager's ethic is the requirement for efficiency, the careful husbanding of resources. For the manager, the scarcity of resources is an all-important fact of life. For the professional, the core ethic is the requirement to apply specialized expertise to get the job done. The limiting resource, for him, is neither material nor fiscal. It is skill and the self-confidence to apply that skill. And because the application of professional skill most often takes place in an environment of uncertainty, the professional practitioner desires slack resources, i.e. more to work with than is prescribed by the parsimonious calculations of the manager. In this case, the requirement for the pilot and his window is not only the result of the self-image of the test pilot. The requirement is also a result of the test pilot's knowledge that the aerospace domain is fraught with uncertainty and that the human mind is the best tool for dealing with surprises. (Another movie that tells of space exploration by human beings, *Apollo 13*, demonstrates the validity of this point.)

The story of the astronauts and the space capsule window is a splendid metaphor for the peril of unhappiness faced by all professionals employed by modern organizations. The

The Problem of Professionalism

universality of this situation is so apparent that it borders on the trite. What physician is not frustrated with the Health Maintenance Organization. What physician does not feel thwarted by the hospital manager's desire to limit the number of tests conducted in a diagnosis procedure? What professor is not perplexed by the Dean's push for higher average class size? What engineer is not irritated by the project manager's concern with limiting the quality of materials purchased? What policeman is not foiled by administrators that restrain his use of force to apprehend criminals?

When I make the point to my students that there is almost always conflict between the manager's concern with efficiency and the professional's concern with producing a desired effect, I throw seven or eight pieces of chalk out of the window. I tell them that the managers (we call them administrators) of the college would be upset with me for doing this because the act is a waste of resource and, after all, the budget is not unlimited, even for the purchase of such mundane items as chalk. On the other hand, because I obviously care about the effective transfer of abstract knowledge from myself to my students more than I care about the chalk bill for the administration, I must be a true professional. I may take pride in sabotaging the aims of the manager, but someday this can come back to haunt me and place me in a position of overt conflict with my organization.

In *The Right Stuff* we see a demonstration of the manner that professionals come into conflict with managers. Now let's take a look at another potential source of unhappiness, one that is caused by conflict between the professional and the society that he seeks to serve.

Neither the professional nor the organization that employs him function in a vacuum. Each is nurtured, either directly or indirectly, by the external (from the perspective of the organized system and the individual practitioner) environment of a society.

Private organizations continue to exist only as long as clients, constituents, or customers demand particular goods and services.

Public organizations exist only with the blessing and the funding of governments. (Remember: "No Buck Rogers, no bucks.")

The individual, the organization, and the society are connected by mechanisms of control. Rules of the game, either explicit or implicit, are established. These are designed to affect the behavior of the expert and produce results that are predictable and (socially) desirable. Mechanisms of control are put into place to thwart a tyranny of expertise. The physician is told to refrain from the use of medicines that are not approved by the Food and Drug Administration, even when in his professional judgment it might be rational to use unproven experimental drugs. The engineer must build to the specifications of a governmentally sanctioned code. The scientist must conform to rules concerning the use of human subjects in experiments. The teacher of young children must eschew corporal punishment, even when the expert teacher knows that a slap on the fanny might be a valuable contribution to the education of the child.

As experts becomes more and more socialized into the isolated confines of their area of narrow practice, it is natural, we might say even inevitable, that they come to believe that they know what is good for society more than the members of society themselves. And this belief is a source of unhappiness for the expert practitioner who wants to put his specialized competence to use at his own discretion.

The stereotypical tough detective portrayed in the film *Dirty Harry* believes that the legal and social constraints of due process are to be avoided for the benefit of society. He plays by his own rules. This cop may be very good at catching and punishing criminals, but in the end he suffers at the hands of those who would control his behavior. In the film *High Noon*, the sheriff rejects the pleas of citizens that the town should avoid a risky confrontation with sociopaths. He is determined to save the town in spite of itself. And even though he guns down the bad guys and marries the beautiful school teacher, the sheriff experiences profound sadness and disillusionment. The architect in the film *The Fountainhead* sees himself as th singular repository of excellence. When he disapproves of the design of a publicly approved and funded housing project, he destroys the buildings by committing a criminal act of arson. His professional standards are higher than the standards of the people who will live in the buildings. His professional standards, however, are the fountainhead of his own agony.

The detective, the sheriff, and the architect in these film stories have all become victims of what, on the one hand, is a highly developed capacity to use a skill that society demands and what, on the other hand, is the self-inflicted wound of zealotry. A dramatic story of the plight of the zealot is told by the movie *A Few Good Men*.

As a result of the 1898 American victory in the Spanish-American war, the United States was given a 99 year renewable lease to build a base at Guantanamo Bay, Cuba. When Fidel Castro became the Cuban leader and declared himself a Marxist, the enclave of the U.S. military base became a hot spot of the Cold War.

The perimeter of the base is lined with a fence manned by stalwart Marines, armed sentries who stand between the free world and the Communist hordes. Of course, the Cubans have an equal number of their own riflemen in position to protect their own world from the pollution of the Americans.

A young Marine, Private Willie Santiago, witnesses one of his comrades taking gratuitous pot shots at his opposite number (mirror) on the Cuban side of the fence. He assumes the role of the whistle blower and reports this violation of the formal rules of engagement: Do not fire unless fired upon.

Such rules are not formulated by the Marine's organization: Rifle Security Company, Marine Barracks Windward, Guantanamo Bay Cuba. They are imposed by higher command. The civilian political arm of the government must control the management of violence. The job of the Marines is to be able to shoot well. The job of the civilian politicians representing American society is to tell Marines when to shoot and who to shoot.

When Private Santiago's complaints are ignored by his Commanding Officer, Colonel Nathan Jessup, Santiago writes to his Congressman. By doing so he ignores the chain-of-command. Private Santiago has violated the informal rules, the code designed to encourage group cohesiveness: Marines do not "rat" on each other; Marines do not go outside of the chain-of-command.

Moreover, shooting at the enemy is not such a bad idea in any event because aggressive behavior demonstrates the presence of the martial spirit.

Because Santiago has behaved so badly, Colonel Jessup must now sanction the young Marine. Jessup is advised by his second-in-command, Lieutenant Colonel Markensen, to ship Santiago back to the mainland. Santiago is in danger, Markensen believes, of bodily harm inflicted by his comrades because he has violated the code.

Jessup rejects this advice. If a Marine shows weakness in any form, his seniors must lead him down the proper path, must make him strong. Colonel Jessup proclaims that "We have a responsibility to this country to see that the men and women charged with its security are trained professionals." "Transfer," he says," is not, in a manner of speaking, the American way!"

Santiago must be taught a lesson and the tool to do this is Code Red, hazing in the form of physical punishment administered by peers. Colonel Jessup orders Lieutenant Kendrick, Santiago's platoon commander, to administer a Code Red. Kendrick surreptitiously passes this order along to Corporal Dawson and Private Downey.

Dawson and Downey push a rag into Santiago's mouth to keep him quiet during the administration of a beating. Santiago, who is not in good shape to start with, suffers an attack of lactic acidosis and dies, drowning in his own blood.

A Navy doctor concludes that Santiago's death must have been the result of poison on the rag stuffed into his mouth by Dawson and Downey.

This is the first step in a coverup designed to protect Colonel Jessup and Lieutenant Kendrick, to protect the Marine Corps. The Colonel and the Lieutenant falsely deny that the Code Red was ordered by them.

The two young marines who were, in fact, following the orders of their seniors, are indicted for murder. The defense

The Problem of Professionalism

lawyer in the court martial of Dawson and Downey is a young Navy Judge Advocate General officer, a recent graduate of Harvard Law School, Lieutenant Junior Grade Caffey.

Caffey is an expert at plea bargaining. In this case, however, he rejects this defense strategy more out of his own hubris than any solid legal logic.

The young Marines plead innocent by virtue of having been given an order originating with Colonel Jessup. If they are found guilty they will spend the rest of their lives in a military prison.

The only witness who can testify that Santiago's death was caused by Colonel Jessup is Lieutenant Colonel Markensen. Jessup's second-in-command is aware of the cover up. But Markensen feels profoundly guilty because he did not protect Santiago by preventing the Code Red action. He feels that his own weakness is the cause of Santiago's death. He commits suicide and Caffey is left without a witness to prove his case.

Lawyer Caffey's only recourse is to call Colonel Jessup to the stand. Jessup has informed Caffey "We are in the business of saving lives." Jessup has told Caffey that he "...eats breakfast 400 yards from Cubans who are trained to kill me."

Caffey perceives that the Colonel's self-image as a valiant and heroic warrior is the chink in his armor. He believes that Jessup is proud of having ordered the Code Red. He feels that Jessup conceives of the Code Red as the right thing to do. Caffey perceives that Jessup believes himself to be not at all vulnerable to the sanctions of the law. He anticipates that Jessup will admit, as he testifies, that he did indeed order the Code Red and he is indeed proud of having done so.

Jessup starts his testimony by claiming that he told Lieutenant Kendrick not to have his men administer a Code Red. He testifies that he told Markenson to have Santiago transferred. Yet Caffey had noticed that Santiago's locker was filled with his personal belongings. He wonders out loud why Santiago was not packed if he was going to be flown to the States early the next morning.

Caffey, who has examined the records of long distance calls from the base, also wonders out loud why Santiago made no calls to tell people he was coming home. These observations are the initial assault on the credibility of the Colonel.

Caffey continues by revealing a lack of logic at the core of the cover up. He asks Jessup whether or not his men always follow orders. The Colonel proudly responds that they do. "Have you ever served in an infantry unit? Put your life in another mans hands?" asks Jessup. "We follow orders or we die."

Caffey asks Jessup to reaffirm that he ordered Lieutenant Kendrick not to use the Code Red sanction. Jessup tells him that is true. Caffey asks Jessup to reaffirm that Kendrick did indeed order his men to refrain from the Code Red. Jessup tells him that is also true. Caffey wonders audibly why, if it is true that Marines always follow orders, and if it is true that there were orders not to give a Code Red, why is it that Dawson and Downey did use the Code Red on Santiago? He asks the rhetoric question, "If you gave an order that he was not to be touched, then why did he have to be transferred?" Colonel Jessup answers weakly, demonstrating the inconsistency of his former assertions, "Sometimes men take matters into their own hands."

"You snotty little bastard!" proclaims the Colonel, sneering at the attacking lawyer. The Colonel's complacency is starting to crumble.

And as this happens Jessup falls back on his paramount source of strength, his professional pride, his expertise, his role of savior of American society. "You cant handle the truth," he says to the lawyer in front of the court martial jury. "We live in a world that has walls and those walls have to be guarded by men with guns. Santiago's death saved lives."

"You want me on that wall!" the Colonel screams. "You need me on that wall!" he shouts. "I have neither the time nor the inclination to explain to a man who rises and sleeps in the blanket of the very freedom I provide and then questions the manner that I provide it. You're goddamned dammed right! I did order the Code Red! I did my job! I would do it again!"

The Problem of Professionalism

The Colonel has confessed to a crime. He is arrested. As a parting shot he says to Lawyer Caffey, "You have no idea how to defend a nation. You put peoples' lives in danger."

As we look at the downfall of Colonel Jessup, we see a clear example of the professional whose dedication to serve results in his incapacity to serve and his inability to experience service as source of happiness.

The case of *A Few Good Men* describes a military organization in a national security situation. Yet we can use the case to understand the substantive problem of the expert in a general way. Society demands, and even craves, the skill of the expert and is often accepting of the narrow view that accompanies such skill. If I have to undergo brain surgery, I do not care if the surgeon understands and is compassionate with the holistic nature of my situation or my humanity. I just want someone that knows exactly how to perform brain surgery.

If I am the passenger on an airliner, I do not care whether or not the pilot accepts the precepts of Judeo-Christian ethics or the ideals of liberal democracy. I just want a pilot who knows how to get me to my destination in one piece.

If I want to be informed by an expert journalist, I want that information to be objective and in full detail.

Yet it will upset me very much if I perceive that: the brain surgeon sees me as a piece of meat to be carved with precision, if the pilot is not sympathetic to the vulnerability I feel as we hit a thunderstorm, if the broadcaster refuses to cater to my desire to be entertained rather than informed.

The expert is confronted with the problem of his own expertise. He is squeezed between the rock of his expertise and the hard place of the holistic needs of those he serves.

Chapter Ten

Fear of the Future:
The cases of *2001- A Space Odyssey, Rollerball*

> "For, after all, how do we know that two and two make four? Or that the force of gravity works, or that the past is unchangeable... If the mind itself is controllable- then what?"
> *1984,* George Orwell

Both the scientist and the artist engage in the process of prediction. The former uses data that can be analyzed to explain what has been observed. Explanation of an observed phenomenon can be used to predict what will occur in the future. When Newton observed the apple fall from the tree and explained this occurrence by suggesting the existence of a force called gravity, he could predict that all objects would behave in the same way as his apple. For the scientist, prediction follows from explanation.

For the artist, explanation follows from prediction. Instead of hard data, the artist uses his imagination. The stories of futures imagined told by movies predict the dangers of possible tomorrows and thereby explain the hazards of today.

Stories that provide us with an image of the future help us to assess the present and thereby to more fully understand the Legend Of The Dysfunctional System.

What imagined future horrors help us understand observable unhappiness of the present? Many stories of the future ask the same question: Is human nature the predominant force, the prime mover, that determines the human condition? And in most stories, the answer is the same. Human nature may have determined the human condition in the past. But the man-made disasters of the past will convince the leaders of the future that the human propensity for self-destruction must be controlled. Human nature, therefore, in the future will no longer determine human destiny. The commanding force of the future, the Legend tells us, will be centrally controlled, machine-like, hierarchically organized systems. These systems will be designed to mitigate the invidious impact of human nature by controlling the behavior of human beings.

The world will become bureaucratized. In the future, according to these stories, strong leaders will realize that man is a fragile, irrational, and imperfect organism, prone to selfishness and error... not at all adept in his quest for happiness.

Film stories of the future tell us that it will become obvious to all that human nature results in the Hobbesian outcome of self-destructive wars of all against all. Typical of such a reality check is the nuclear holocaust that precedes the action in the movie based on Orwell's famous novel, *1984*.

To escape from the nastiness of such a condition, arrangements will be made that remedy the situation by controlling human behavior for its own good. Since nature has produced man as an imperfect being, it becomes the task of man to establish centrally managed artificial systems that override nature and thereby control human behavior. The design of the man-made organized system will be the responsibility of those few elites who know better what is good for the human condition than does the common natural wisdom of mankind.

The consequence of such remedies is a paradox, we are told. The attempt to perfect the condition of mankind by developing machine-like systems will result in profound distress for human beings, i.e. the imperfect organic parts of the system. In many stories of the future, the cure, order, is worse than the disease, freedom.

The paradox of a machine-like system composed of human organic parts is illuminated by the story told in the movie *2001, A Space Odyssey*. This movie tells the tale of a group of astronauts sent from earth to Jupiter on an important mission. There is a good possibility that intelligent life exits on that planet and the crew of the spaceship has been sent to explore the possibility. The dominant decision maker on board is an advanced computer named HAL. HAL has been programed, i.e. trained, to navigate the spaceship to its destination and to solve problems that may be encountered on the journey. HAL has also been programed to learn: to modify its program as it confronts situations not anticipated by the original data input. The audience is encouraged to accept the idea that HAL is programmed not just with factual knowledge, but also with values that hold mission accomplishment to be of the highest priority.

During the flight towards Jupiter, HAL decides to take over the space ship, to mutiny by destroying the spaceship's human crew. The focus of this part of the drama is the battle of wits in a life and death struggle between HAL and the last remaining live human on board, Dave.

What is the motivation of the computer to take such radical action? Has the machine merely run amok? Perhaps there is more to it than that.

At the core of the high drama in the battle for control between HAL and Dave is the logic that results from the computer's knowledge of facts and its perception of the supreme value of the mission. The computer knows that a machine of its advanced design has never made an error. HAL also knows that human beings have, indeed, made errors. From the perspective of the computer, therefore, the probability of mission success will be enhanced if the human crew is destroyed and the computer takes over.

This is the converse of the tale of mutiny aboard the U.S.S. Caine described in Chapter Seven. In the film *2001*, the machine, HAL, does not trust the decision effectiveness of the human, Dave. In *The Caine Mutiny*, the human, Steve Maryk, does not trust the decision effectiveness of Captain Queeg. Queeg has been socialized, or programmed, to take on the values of the machine-like bureaucracy. Queeg has become the personification of the organization. He insists on conforming to the standard procedures and to the hierarchical structure programmed into the organization just has HAL conforms to the data that determines its behavior.

Whether the man or the organization-machine is better equipped to deal with the complexities and uncertainties of the situations described in *2001* and *The Caine Mutiny* is not at issue here. What is at issue, is the pattern of events that is part of the Legend Of The Dysfunctional System, a pattern that tells us what can happen when a machine-like system is composed of organic (i.e.human) parts. This is a pattern of mutiny, the overt manifestation of conflict between the organization and its members, the transition from the organizational promise of order and stability to the actuality of conflict and chaos.

When organic-man confronts machine-system, the human is presented with a problem that is intrinsic to his very being. He loves freedom, but he does not have the capacity to use his freedom in a way that consistently results in his own happiness. Freedom makes him vulnerable to treading paths that lead to unhappiness. The function of the machine-system presented in stories of the future is to provide man with choices that are severely limited, to allow him only those choices that will result in his own happiness, to stifle his freedom. Such stories are based on the assumption of leaders that the elite controllers of the machine-system have exclusive access to the wisdom that produces human happiness. (Remember the picture of a utopia painted by Mr. Jensen in the movie Network described in Chapter Three.)

The controllers of the machine-system assume that freedom and happiness are mutually exclusive choices; if you gain one, you lose the other. This notion presents us with a cruel dilemma.

Freedom seems to be one of those conditions that man values for itself. And something that is a valued end in and of itself represents, according to Aristotle's conception, a condition of happiness. Freedom may not be a sufficient condition for happiness, but it is a necessary condition. Stories of the future that are part of the Legend tell that if we allow man the means of free choice, the result will be unhappiness. But if we take away freedom, man seeks it as an end in itself. The story told by the movie Rollerball, which describes the relationship of a hero to his organization, is a vivid depiction of this dilemma.

The movie *Rollerball* describes a world where nations are no longer the basic unit of earthly society. This is presumably the result of disastrous world wars. Reorganization of the global structure was initially based on corporations. (Once again think about Mr. Jensen in *Network*.) But a world structure based on many corporations was too fragmented. Competition looked uncomfortably like tribal warfare. So the fragmented pieces were integrated into functional Divisions, The Majors: Transport, Food, Finance, Communications, Energy, Housing. The executive leaders of these divisions make up the Board of Directors that controls the world. These few executives make all decisions for the common good. Each functional Division has its corporate headquarters in an urban center:Energy in Houston, Food in Chicago, Communications in Tokyo etc.

Now everyone is comfortable. All material needs are provided. Beyond the basic needs, there are many luxuries available to all. The Corporate System takes care of everyone. All the Corporate leaders ask is that people do not question or interfere with management decisions.

Many stories of the future predict the coming of highly integrated centralized systems of human control. George Orwell's *1984* is a classic of this genre. In *1984* the competition between the few units of the global structure results in continuous warfare. Eurasia, Eastasia and Oceania fight constantly. The leaders of these multi-continent giants control their own societies by referring to external threats and by the use of psychological and technological tools of manipulation. Big Brother is always watching.

The uniqueness of the movie *Rollerball* is the manner in which the problem of competition among the mega-units (Energy, Communication, etc.) and the resultant aggressiveness of the units themselves is resolved. There is always the possibility that cooperation among the few executives will break down and that there will be irrational economic competition, political strife, or even military war. Sport, however, has become the substitute for all forms of harmful competition, including war. The sport is called Rollerball.

A Rollerball field of play is laid out inside a massive arena located in each city that hosts a Major functional corporate unit. A slick oval banked surface provides a track around which the players, some on roller skates, some on small motorcycles, can circle at great speed. The action starts when an official controller launches a heavy melon sized ball onto the floor of the track. The object of the game is for a player to pick up the ball and sink it into a pipe that is the trackside goal. Skating players use the hitch-handle on the back of teammates' cycles to speed up their progress around the track. As opposing team members attempt to gain control of the ball and sink it in the pipe, the action is fast and furious and loaded with violence. Defending against a goalward bound player often means bashing the skating or cycling opponent and doing great bodily harm.

The violence on the track is reflected in the excited attitude of the fans. Fan loyalty here goes beyond the ordinary identification with a team. It springs from a deep sense of patriotism and chauvinism: devotion to a cause.

The Rollerball season ends when the best teams compete for the world championship. The defending champion this year is Houston.

Rollerball players occupy a unique place in society. They are a combination of Knights in Shining Armor and Gladiators. They represent the marshal spirit. They protect the honor of their cities. They also provide an outlet for the aggressive disposition of the citizenry.

Skating for the Houston team is Jonathan E. Jonathan is the best Rollerball player in the world, a hero of heroes. He has had a long and distinguished career. Rollerball, it seems, is his life, and a good life it seems to be. Jonathan lives in the lap of luxury. He is adored and admired by all, including the series of young and beautiful women that, at the direction of Houston executives, have shared his ranch-mansion since the mysterious departure, years ago, of his wife.

Houston is nearing its goal of another championship season. But first they have to beat Tokyo and then New York.

Mr. Bartholomew is the Executive Director of the Houston Corporation. He is having a hard time thinking up rewards that will continue to motivate Jonathan. Jonathan has everything he needs. Bartholomew decides to put on a special multivision show that will tell Jonathan's heroic story.This will stroke Jonathan's ego.

But there is more to Jonathan's situation than the need for ego stroking. He is told that there are executives that want him out of the game. He has had ten years. He is perceived by executive leaders to be a threat because he commands such dedicated fan loyalty. Some of the executives want the special multivision program planned by Bartholomew to be used to announce Jonathan's retirement. An old friend tells Jonathan, "They are afraid of you... all the way to the top they are." Bartholomew wants Jonathan to retire. He tells Jonathan that "No player is greater than the game itself...It is not a game a man is supposed to grow strong in."

Jonathan's life energy is totally devoted to his role as a player in the game. He desires neither more fame nor fortune nor power. Jonathan points out that the team depends on him. Bartholomew tells him that the game serves a social purpose as a substitute for aggressive competitiveness and that this is more important than the needs of Jonathan which are fulfilled by his participation as a player. Bartholomew fails to appreciate Jonathan's point of view and tells him that if he does not retire willingly, he will be forced into retirement.

Now the Houston team faces Tokyo. The executive leadership has decided that in this game there will be no penalties and only limited substitution for injured players. The rules have been changed to make the game more violent, more interesting to the crowd and more dangerous for Jonathan and his teammates.

Bartholomew tells Jonathan that he is not to play against Tokyo or ever again. The Houston executive is embarrassed by the multivision event where Jonathan failed to announce his retirement. Jonathan is told that if he retires, his future comfort is assured. The Energy Corporation will treat him well. But Jonathan wants more than ever to play. He defies the powers that be and plays in the game. Like Sonny Steele, in the movie *Electric Horseman*, Jonathan detaches himself from the corporation to satisfy the needs of the role that drives him from within.

In the Tokyo game, Houston's opponent takes an initial 1 to 0 lead. There is much violence. Jonathan scores and ties the game. Many players are injured. There are frequent violations of the old rules that had been designed to prevent serious injury. But the old rules do not apply. In this game there are no penalties for excessive violence. The game turns into a melee and Jonathan's best friend is so severely injured that he is pronounced brain dead. Jonathan mauls an opposing player and then scores the winning goal. The crowd goes wild.

Houston will play New York for the world championship. But before the game a problem has to be resolved. The Board of Directors, consisting of the leaders of each Corporation, are in conflict with Bartholomew. He has lost control of Jonathan E. This creates an intolerable situation. Bartholomew agrees that Jonathan is an obstacle to world stability. He proposes that in the next game there will be no rules, no substitutions for injured players and no time limit. The game will be played in conditions of anarchy. Given Jonathan's drive to win, he will probably sacrifice his life for the good of the team. There will be no accidents, nothing suspicious. "Let the game do its work," Bartholomew tells his fellow Directors. The game, indeed, he points out, "...was created to demonstrate the futility of the individual. If a champion defeats the meaning for which the game is designed, then he must lose." The Directors vote to go ahead with Bartholomew's plan of an anarchic game. This is a plan designed to bring about the demise of Jonathan.

We witness the championship game, Houston vs. New York. If there is no limit on the time played, how can you have a winner? The answer is that they will play until all players die, including Jonathan.Thus, Bartholomew's problem of a recalcitrant powerful underling will be solved.

The violence begins. A player is thrown into the blood thirsty crowd and beaten. Jonathan continues to play effectively despite being beaten by others. The crowd turns against him and chants, "Jonathan is dead!"

The Houston coach tells his players "This was not meant to be a game...never."

Neither team has scored. There are injured and dead players spread over the field of play. Jonathan is on the track faced by two remaining opponents, one with a motorcycle and one on skates. Jonathan breaks the neck of the New York skater right in front of Bartholomew. The cyclist goes after Jonathan. It is now one-on-one, mano-a- mano. Jonathan has the New York player down and can kill him by bashing him with ball. The crowd is silent. Jonathan takes off his helmet. He stares at Bartholomew. He places the ball in the goal. Houston has won the world championship. The crowd chants, "Jonathan!!! Jonathan!!!" The hero circles the arena. He is in his glory.

The movie *Rollerball* reminds us that an imaginative look into the future can help us to understand some of the fundamental problems of the present. Just as in the movie *Lost in America*, the protagonist is confronted with choices that can lead to either freedom or comfort, or some combination of both. In *Lost in America*, David and Linda chose to sacrifice some freedom for the comfort that the advertising agency could provide. Jonathan,however,eschews comfort to assert his freedom to be what he is: a Rollerball player.

In the world of *Rollerball*, the active process of conflict has been eliminated and replaced with the surrogate of sport. A worldwide bureaucracy has been created. The needs of the group/system far override the needs of the individual. An attempt has been made to replace freedom with comfort as the end in itself that can be experienced as happiness. The few are expected to sacrifice themselves for the many, for the common (sic) good. Like the airmen in the movie *Twelve O'clock High* the players in the game that has no constraint on violence, and no time limit, are all expected to die for the good of the system. Here, the system is dramatically dysfunctional for the individual.

Chapter Eleven

Coping Strategies: Directing Your Movie

> "There's one part of the workplace that nobody but you is the boss of and that's your own state of mind, your own effort, where you're putting your attention."
> *Work as a Spiritual Practice*, Lewis Richmond

The Legend Of The Dysfunctional System tells us that harmony between an organization and its members is fragile. This fragility is a fact of organizational life, built into the structural conditions that describe the relationship between the system and its parts. The individual is always vulnerable to the slings and arrows that can inflict pain, unhappiness, and disillusionment.

Each of the stories that are part of the Legend takes place in a different context. Yet, in each of the stories one or more of the actors experiences a wake up call that informs him unambiguously that there is very real conflict between himself and his organization.

Max learns that UBS is no longer a useful professional home. Lieutenant Bishop discovers that to be a man he must die.

Jonathan E. finds out that the Houston Corporation is using him for its own ends. Sonny Steele ascertains that his organization has uncowboyed him... etc. etc.

In each of these stories we are advised of a specific problem in the context of a particular circumstance, a problem that is a manifestation of the ubiquitous condition of fragile harmony.

The Legend, however, does not only describe problems. It also suggests solutions that take the form of coping strategies. These can take one or a combination of the following forms:

-Face a reality that is not ideal and make the best of it.
-Change the problematic reality.
-Exit the problematic reality.

The optimal relationship between the organized system and its human parts is one of common of purpose. This happy circumstance can be experienced for some period of time. David and his advertising firm are on the same track for eight years. But his train runs off the track when he is informed that he will not be promoted to Executive Vice President. He copes at first by escaping from the corporation and finally by accepting a role that provides him with some of the rewards of corporate life and at the same time deprives him of that illusive gold ring. His new role, taking on the Ford account in New York, is not optimal. It is satisfactory. Optimally, he would be Executive Vice President. Yet David's decision to go to New York brings him one step closer to happiness than he was as the disappointed executive or as the overqualified crossing guard.

The Legend tells us that coping is an incremental process, that organizational life is best experienced as a journey and not as a destination.

The starting point for our exploration of the Legend was Aristotle's notion that happiness is derived from the satisfaction experienced as a result of activity that is an end in itself. It follows from this, he tells us, that an individual is happy, or that he is not happy, only at the very end of his life.

We initiate activity as a means to an end. This end becomes another means to another end. In the final analysis how can we know what the end is before we get to the very end of the journey? Film stories help us to transpose these philosophical and abstract notions into something more tangible.

Most of us would reject the idea that we should not be concerned with an evaluation of our own happiness until our life is at an end. It would make more sense to imagine our lives as increments of experience, discrete segments of means and ends that can be lived, evaluated, and perhaps shifted in new directions constructed of new segments of means and ends.

Sonny Steele conceived of his rodeo success as an end in itself. He was a happy cowboy. When aging and injury made it clear that rodeo success could only be a means to the goal of a steady job, he took the job and for a time lived high on the hog. After a while his wake up call, in the form of the awareness of the plight of the horse Rising Star, caused him to see his job as way of making contact with the horse. And the horse became a means of escape to whatever ends waited for him in the future. When he frees Rising Star to go back to nature and when he walks off into the setting sun, he has no idea where the next stop is. But he does know that he has shifted the course of his journey.

Happiness is approached and not achieved. Abraham Maslow's idea of self-actualization (Maslow 1954) implies the same concept.

Coping, then, is the process of approaching happiness by making adjustments in response to the reality that one faces at any given time, a reality that is determined by the dynamics of our own particular situations, by our own particular individuality and by the stages of life through which we all proceed.

Situational dynamics, individuality, and progress through the stages of life represent an infinite variety of variables that can be blended into an inestimable variety of stories, a variety of life experiences. There is, therefore, no single formula that prescribes a perfect coping strategy. The Legend tells us that there is a broad scope of strategies that can be used by a wide range of individual personalities in an extensive spectrum of circumstances. It does not suggest a singular solution to the fundamental problem. The Legend teaches lessons that offer choices. Let's look at the options.

The fundamental choice is between conformity and alienation. Each of these contains a spectrum of strategies for coping.

A coping strategy of conformity involves an attempt to link individual values to the systemic purposes of the organization. This necessitates some degree of acceptance of the organization's formal mission and its goal of survival. But this does not mean blind acceptance, surrender. It does not mean giving up on the idea that one purpose of the organization can be the satisfaction of individual needs. Indeed, conformity as coping involves using whatever the organization can provide to satisfy individual human needs.

One strategy of conformity is that of personal transformation. Here the character eschews changing the organization's perspective. Instead he changes himself in a way that, ultimately, will bring him one step closer to where he (probably) wanted to be in the first place. He changes for his own good. And the organization itself can provide the impetus for such a change.

As has been noted in Chapter Four, in the move *Twelve O'clock High*, Lieutenant Ben Gaitley is the Air Executive Officer. He is in charge of all the flying operations of the 918th Bomber Group. He has more experience than any other pilot with respect to time flying large four engine planes. Moreover, he is the son of one fine General and the grandson of another.

His wake up call comes when his new commanding officer, General Savage, realizes that Gaitley schedules himself to stay on the ground rather than to join the more junior pilots on very dangerous missions. Savage recognizes in Gaitely a "...yellow streak a mile wide." Gaitley's cowardice has put him in direct conflict with what Savage sees as the purpose of the organization. Savage has Gaitely

Coping Strategies: Directing Your Movie

relieved of his duties as Air Executive Officer. He assigns him as pilot in command of a B17 bomber the crew of which will consist of all the screw ups in the organization. And the name of the aircraft is to be "The Leper Colony".

This is a risky decision for Savage. His action may result in the certain demise of this newly formed weak crew. Yet Savage is willing to bet that the effectiveness of a weak crewman will be improved by his knowledge that the survival of all depends on the performance of each. And in the case of Gaitley, this works. Gaitley accepts his new role as a pilot who flys every mission. As he does so, he becomes transformed. He changes from coward to hero.

When Gaitley's plane is damaged and he has to crash in the English Channel he is rescued. His back is broken. He is hospitalized with a very painful injury.

As he lies in bed in agony, Savage asks him if he needs anything. With his eyes starting to water, not with pain but with joy, Gaitley replies, "That's O.K. General, I have everything I need."

If we looked at this part of the story as a lesson in leadership we would analyze and perhaps praise the leadership of Savage, who found a way to reconcile the needs of the organization with the needs of the individual.

Yet Gaitley is no mechanical cog in the organizational machinery, a cog to be greased and fine tuned by his leader. Gaitley is a living organism with a heart, a brain and a soul. He has choices, not the least of which is the option to remove himself from flying status. He could have responded to the wake up call by quitting his assignment as a flying officer. He would then be reassigned outside of the 918th Bomber Group. When he rejects this choice, when he accepts Savage's challenge, he starts on the path of self-transformation.

As we observe Gaitley's behavior we can see one way that notions about leadership can be turned on their head to become notions of individual coping. As has been pointed out in Chapter Two, C.I. Barnard suggested that leaders should, as much as possible, confine their directives to a follower's zone of indifference. (Barnard 1938) For Barnard, this meant a zone where the organization does not have to use organizational resources to encourage cooperation. The leader effects cooperation without the use of organizational resource because the follower is indifferent to the performance of the required duties.

The width of an individual's zone of indifference at any given time depends on the extent of socialization that has been completed. And we usually, along with Barnard, conceive of socialization and of the issuing of appropriate directives as a leadership function. The effective leader not only issues appropriate directives, he also attempts to widen a follower's zone of indifference by encouraging an increasing depth of socialization. An infinitely wide zone of indifference would mean that a follower would be indifferent to the carrying out of *any* order. A happy circumstance from the perspective of the leader.

The idea of coping in Gaitley's case, however, depends on the capacity of the follower to control the width of his own zone of indifference. Prior to his wake up call, Gaitley's zone of indifference was quite narrow. He was not at all indifferent to the implication that, given his job description, he was required to be an active flyer even in the face of near certain death. When he opts to accept assignment as the pilot in command of "The Leper Colony" he is in effect saying that he is in control of his own zone of indifference. He is willing to widen the zone, to accept orders that were anathema to him in the past.

Leadership involves control of subordinates. Coping in the form of personal transformation involves self control.

Another form of conformity as a coping mechanism involves using the organization as a vehicle for an individual's rite of passage. As a person accumulates on-the-job experience he becomes mature with respect to the functions that he performs, he learns to be effective at his work.

Furthermore, the complexities of the technical and human interactions he experiences can encourage him to become mature with respect to living an effective, one might even say happy, life. The organization can provide a bridge for a

Coping Strategies:Directing Your Movie

passage from a state of immaturity to a condition of maturity.

In the movie *The Caine Mutiny*, Willie Keith is a recent college graduate faced with the prospect of being drafted into the Army to join American forces fighting in World War II. Willie is the son of very wealthy parents, the father a physician, the mother an overbearing dowager.

Willie's father, although professionally successful, has never matured sufficiently to stand up to his dominating wife. In his personal life, Willie's father always takes the easy way out. It is clear that Willie, at age 21, is in danger of following in his father's footsteps. Instead of becoming a foot soldier, Willie uses his family's influence to join the Navy and become an officer.

Willie has two immediate problems. His family connections and his talent as a piano player and singer of songs has landed him a safe, soft job working for an Admiral ashore in Hawaii. Willie will spend most of his time at the Officer's Club. He is safe and comfortable, having avoided the unpleasantness of the war. But his self-esteem is suffering and he is in danger of becoming stuck in the role of dilettante post-adolescent.

His second problem has to do with the fact that he has fallen in love with a lovely young woman, May. May is Italian and quite lower class. There is no way that Willie's mother is going to accept May. Willie is in danger of playing the role of snob and rejecting the love of his life.

Willie's first step on his rite of passage takes the classic form of escaping by going to sea. Willie decides to quit the soft life. He requests a transfer to combat duty aboard a ship. This decision launches him on a course of experiences, a series of means and ends, which result in a passage to maturity.

At first, Willie is completely green with respect to the day to day process of serving as a seagoing officer aboard the U.S.S. Caine. He becomes sick when he climbs the ship's mast as part of the new officer indoctrination procedure. He stuffs a crucial radio message in his pocket and forgets to deliver it. He is unmercifully slow at decrypting secret messages.

Willie is also green with respect to dealing with the

complexities of human interaction that he observes and experiences aboard the Caine. He fails to appreciate the worthiness of his first commanding officer, a man who pays little attention to navy formality, but who is a proficient seaman and leader.

When his second commanding officer, the neurotic Captain Queeg, comes aboard, Willie believes a new day of organizational effectiveness has dawned. Queeg is a stickler for the details of navy discipline (protocol, haircuts, shoe shines, uniforms) even when there is no relevance of these to the wartime circumstances and mission of the Caine. Willie is taken in by all this.

As his fellow officer's become disillusioned with Captain Queeg in general and in particular with his lack of skill as a seaman, Willie's perception swings so as to value the opinion of the cynical and self-serving novelist-officer, Lieutenant Keefer. Willie is like a straw in the wind, shifting with the vagaries of the moment. A series of crises, however, provides Willie with one wake up call after another. This process pushes him toward maturity.

Willie receives a long delayed letter from his father. By the time the letter arrives Willie's father is already dead of cancer. His father knows he is dying and wants to provide Willie with the benefit of his own life experience. Willie's father tells him that he regrets never having stood up on his own two feet. He knows that he had choices to make, particularly with respect to accepting subservience to his wife. He knows, but he knows too late, that this was a mistake. He does not want Willie to use him as a role model. The events that follow provide Willie with ample opportunity to reexamine himself and to look to his shipboard environment for lessons to learn and for people to accept or reject as role models.

Close upon the heels of his father's revelations concerning the necessity for individual strength of character, Willie becomes disillusioned by the crisis of Captain Queeg's failure as a leader. Queeg is a tyrant and not at all the savior that Willie had once pictured. His commanding officer has lost the confidence of the crew and has blundered his way into one mishap after another. Willie learns that there is more to success than merely enforcing the external manifestations of discipline.

When the Caine is threatened by a typhoon and when Queeg's skill and nerve fail, Willie joins his Executive Officer, Steve Maryk, in replacing the Captain to save the ship. As Willie observes the professional and personal destruction of Queeg at Maryk's court martial, Willie is encouraged to wonder about the morality of his decision to participate in what might have been as much a mutiny as an act of heroism. He wonders whether or not Queeg's failure was the result of the failure of the ship's officers to support rather than resist their captain's efforts at leading the crew and operating the ship.

Finally, Willie witnesses the cowardice of Lieutenant Keefer. Over time Keefer becomes the commanding officer of the Caine. When the ship is attacked by suicide-bent Japanese pilots, Keefer deserts the damaged ship. Willie takes over and by the end of the war is tasked, as the last commanding officer of the Caine, to bring the ship home.

Willie's wartime experience has indeed been a rite of passage. By war's end he is not only the commanding officer of the ship, he is also in command of his own fate.

He has come into conflict with his organization, the Navy in general, the Caine under Queeg in particular. He was not always the central actor at the vortex of the organizational storms experienced aboard the Caine. But he was a close observer. The Caine became a school for Willie, not only where he would learn the lessons of the organization, but also where he would learn the lessons of life.

In the end, Willie rejects the dominance of his mother and marries May. In the end, Willie has coped with conflict by using the heat of conflict to forge his own maturity.

A third variety of conformity as a coping mechanism suggests that followers resolve conflict by helping leaders. (Chaleff 1998) This involves neither personal transformation nor a rite of passage. Rather, it entails finding a way to be loyal to the organization and at the same time maintain loyalty to yourself.

The role of Major Harvey Stoval in *Twelve O'clock High* is an archetypical example of this coping strategy. Stoval is the Ground Executive Officer. He has control over the administrative apparatus of the bomber group: files, correspondence, personnel records etc. He has been around since the inception of the 918th and is knowledgeable concerning the capabilities and attitudes of all personnel.

General Frank Savage is new to the group and depends on Stoval for information and for the administrative tools necessary to lead. Stoval admires his former Commanding Officer and close friend, Colonel Keith Davenport. He resents Davenport's replacement by the seemingly harsh and unfeeling General Savage.

Quite naturally, Stoval resists cooperating with Savage. When Savage asks Stoval's advice concerning the choice of an Air Executive Officer to replace the disgraced Gaitley, Stoval replies, "I'm sure the General will find any of the pilots satisfactory." In effect, Stoval is telling his boss to go to hell in much the same way that David in *Lost in America* responded to his boss's directive to go to New York to work on the Ford account. Stoval is in conflict with his organization and the days ahead seem bleak.

To cope with the situation, Stoval will take action that helps his leader. Unlike David, Stoval does not have to transform himself to effect a happy adaptation to an unhappy circumstance.

In civilian life, Stoval was a lawyer. He is used to the role of advocate, a role based on the value of advising, assisting, and in general helping others. Unlike Willie Keith in *The Caine Mutiny*, Stoval does not have to become mature to cope with the situation at hand or with life in general. He is older than most people in the bomber group, a veteran of World War I, in his own words, a "retread." Stoval's life experience has resulted in his adopting an attitude of sincere patriotism. His loyalty to the cause of victory as well as his values as an advocate tell us that his anger with Savage is more a mood than a meaningful conflict between his values and the mission and/

or well being of the 918th. What he does do to cope with this conflict, indeed to resolve it, is to rid himself of the disappointment concerning the professional ruin of his friend, Colonel Davenport. And as he does this he emphasizes the lawyer-advocate role. He takes on the 918th Bomber Group as a client.

On a day when heavy rain and low visibility has resulted in canceled flight operations, Savage is busy with paper work. Stoval calls him on the intercom. "I've made some fresh coffee, General. Would you like me to bring you a cup?" "No, Harvey. Stay put. I'll come and get it," says Savage. The General, by refusing to be served by Stoval, and by calling him by his first name, implicitly recognizes that he needs Stoval for an ally if he is to lead effectively. As they sip coffee together Stoval advises his General concerning the attitudes and capabilities of the men in the group. This is exactly the sort of help Savage needs.

Savage, however, has more severe problems than the need for information. He has given his pilots an opportunity to request a transfer from flying status if they are unwilling to continue on a path to almost certain death. Savage sees this ploy as a challenge that the men will accept, a challenge to continue flying for the cause of victory. But the men don't see it that way. They all process the forms required to initiate a withdrawal from flying status. This will mean the end of the 918th Bomber Group and the end of Savage's career.

Savage needs time to work with the men to develop some pride in meaningful accomplishment. This will encourage them to withdraw their transfer requests. Stoval helps him accomplish just that.

The written requests for transfer must be reviewed by Stoval for accuracy and form. Then they must be forwarded to higher headquarters. Stoval decides to stonewall the paper work. He will agonize for days, perhaps weeks, over dotting each *i* and crossing each *t*. This will give Savage the time he needs. "I don't know, Harvey," warns General Savage, "there may be trouble for you in this." Stoval brushes the warning aside by proclaiming that he never heard of "...a jury convicting the lawyer."

Stoval has resolved the conflict between his own initial purpose, thwarting his General, and the mission of his organization. He has done so by realizing that by helping the organization he helps himself, he satisfies the values that define his authentic role, that of mature advocate.

Not all coping mechanisms call for cooperation and conformity. The Legend suggests a second possible general approach to coping with conflict. This is a strategy that dictates various degrees of alienation. Here the actors assume roles that reject organizational values or structure in ways that vary from mild to extreme.

The mildest prescription for alienation as coping suggests that the individual embrace the role of creative rebel. Here, the rules and norms of the organization are violated to create a situation where individual and system purpose are moved closer to a state of harmony. In effect, the individual makes up his own rules. Yet the rebellion is creative in the sense that it is not intended to wreck or even diminish the organization's progress toward its goals. Creative rebellion is not sabotage. When neither rules nor statements of mission can fully capture the dynamics and complexities of the organizational setting, creative rebellion can be beneficial for both the organization and the individual.

In the film *Local Hero*, Mr. Happer is the CEO of Knox Oil and Gas Corporation. The mission of the organization is to make a profit by discovering, drilling, refining and selling oil. Happer wants to procure land in Scotland on which to build a North Sea oil storage and refining facility. This would result in greater profits.

Happer is not at all satisfied by his role as business executive. He is a serious amateur astronomer. He dreams of discovering a comet that can be named after him.

When Happer learns, first hand, of the environmental vulnerability of the land that his organization is bent on purchasing and of the resistance of the owner of exceptionally beautiful beach front property to sell, he rebels creatively. Happer abandons plans for the oil storage and refining facility and decides, rather, to construct a world class land, sea and sky environmental study center. In doing so, Happer has violated the norms of Knox Oil and Gas. This is an energy company, not an environmental company. Yet his decision concerning the land in Scotland will not impact dramatically on company profits. The company is just too big for that. We can imagine that good environmental deeds will, in the long run, help the company maintain its position of strength and profitability. More important, from the point of view of Happer's problem of lack of enthusiasm concerning the profit norms of Knox Oil and Gas, Happer has maintained his position as CEO and brought about change that moves him closer to a state of harmony with the organization.

In Chapter Four we saw that General Savage, in *Twelve O'clock High*, also assumes the role of creative rebel. His boss, General Pritchard, sends out a radio message to recall all aircraft that are proceeding toward targets which are obscured by bad weather. Pritchard does not want to risk valuable assets in circumstances where the probability of gain is low. This puts Savage in conflict with the necessity to follow the rules and to conform to the norm of following orders.

At this point in the story Savage has whipped his aircrews into shape. He needs a successful mission to develop the pride and confidence that will motivate his men to press on with their flying duties. He needs to continue with the mission in the face of orders from headquarters to return. Savage fakes radio failure. If he never receives the radio message from General Pritchard, he can, he believes, put some bombs on target and thereby help the organization and help himself to maintain his position as commander of his bomber group. He accomplishes his purpose with a successful mission and in the long run enhances the accomplishments of the Army Air Corps. But to do this he had to eschew playing by the rules. By rebelling creatively he creates a win-win situation for himself and for his organization.

Not all strategies of alienation result in scenarios where both the individual and the organization come out ahead. Sometimes the story is one where push comes to shove. The individual and the organization are playing a zero sum game; what one wins, the other loses.

Most of the time, organizations hold the power cards and

control the resources needed by the individual. One form of alienation as coping is designed to turn the tables. The individual acts as a more or less free agent. He exercises options that had not been viable as long as he believed that he was dependent on the organization. He becomes an uncooperative rebel. In the film *Network*, Max takes this option.

One of the many crises in this story focuses on Max's alienation from the organization due to his loyalty to Howard. As has been noted in Chapter Three, Howard has been vacillating back and forth between wanting to maintain his role as a professional journalist and wanting to become the willing puppet of the organization by acting more as an entertainer than as a reporter. The tension between these two roles and the pressure for higher ratings results in Howard's nervous breakdown and absurd behavior while on the air. Given one last chance to behave according to the dictates of the organization (United Broadcasting System) Howard loses control and rants and raves concerning all he feels is wrong with modern civilization, with television, and with his fellow human beings. Max, who is Howard's boss, is monitoring the broadcast in the control booth. A call comes in for the people controlling the show's transmission. Network superiors order that Howard be cut off the air in mid-sentence. Max countervenes the order as he exclaims, "Leave him on!"

Max has provided his friend with a forum to go out in a blaze of glory. But he has placed the Network in an extremely embarrassing situation. His superiors demand Max's resignation.

In a movie closer to fact than to fiction, *The Right Stuff*, the character John Glenn, described in Chapter Nine, also acts as an uncooperative rebel. All of the original astronauts feel threatened. They may lose their status as pilots to achieve status as spacemen. An aircraft needs a pilot. A spacecraft, at least according to early NASA high level administrators and scientists, does not. Most of the functions to be performed can accomplished remotely by ground controllers or by internal automated systems. Indeed the first living "American" in space was a chimpanzee.

When the seven Mercury astronaut view the prototype

capsule they observe that the design does not include a window. They become very upset. Without a window they are merely "Span in the can". Glenn realizes that the purpose of the human in the space capsule is as much political as technical. The President has promised the American people that the nation will put a man on the moon, thereby beating the Soviets at that accomplishment. The political purpose of the space program conflicts with technical and administrative criteria of the moment.

Instead of accepting a windowless space capsule, Glen rebels by informing his seniors that there will be no "Buck Rogers" without a window. And without "Buck Rogers" there will be no "bucks" coming into NASA from Congress. Glen and his fellows will walk out on the project. Unlike the United Broadcasting System in *Network*, here the organization gives in. Glenn and his comrades have their way. A window is put into the design. The loser here is NASA and its senior engineers, who desire a windowless capsule because it will be more structurally sound, and its senior administrators, who desire a windowless capsule because it will be more cost-effective.

The results of uncooperative alienation are indeterminate. Max rebelled and thereby saved his dignity, but lost his job. Glenn saved his dignity and his job as well. As the severity of rebellion increases, so does the risk. Clearly, the characters here have to make decisions concerning the tradeoff between happiness and job security. The Legend tells us that the path to happiness is often obscured by the lure of job security. The various options of alienation suggested by the Legend become increasingly severe. Next, we look at the strategy of martyrdom. Here the individual sacrifices himself to accomplish some objective that is considered to be supremely valuable.

In the film *Silkwood*, Karen Silkwood chooses this path. She is devoted to the cause of protecting her fellow employees (and herself) from deadly radiation, radiation that the firm is willing to ignore to pursue its goal of profit. Karen's rebellious persistence places her in the path of danger. Her boyfriend, Drew, who works at the same plant, decides to quit and head for greener pastures. He is no martyr. Karen decides to stay on and to work with union officials and with government regulators to prove that the company action is not only immoral, but illegal. Karen is exposed to radiation and will probably suffer the consequences.

But Karen does not live long enough to fall victim to the cancer that would result from overexposure to radiation. She is killed in an automobile accident. The plot of the film strongly suggests that Karen's death was no accident. It appears as though she was murdered by those who could not tolerate her interference in company policy. Karen has, perhaps unwittingly, sacrificed her life in the cause of justice for the workers in the nuclear energy industry.

The behavior of Lieutenant Bishop, in *Twelve O'clock High*, also demonstrates the strategy of the martyr. Bishop assumes this roll because he considers his status as a man and the mission of the Bomber Group to be of utmost importance. The linking of his manhood with his role as combat pilot results in his death.

Finally, the Legend reveals the coping strategy of exit. Here the individual seeks neither to change himself, nor to change the situation, but rather to separate himself from the system with which he is in conflict.

Sonny Steel, in *Electric Horseman*, climbs aboard Rising Star and literally flees from everything that has caused him to become disgusted with himself. By attaching himself to the corporation, he was running away from his authentic self. Ultimately, he decides to stop doing that and to run away from the corporation.

The sheriff in the film *High Noon* also selects a strategy of exit. When violent criminals approach to do him harm, the people of the town reject his cry for help. He stays and fights, approaching the status of martyr.

Yet when the bad guys are dispatched, he rides out of town (like Sonny Steele) accompanied by his bride, to an unknown future.

The end of the film *Local Hero* places Mac in a more gentle, but nevertheless compelling, circumstance. Mac's experience in the small Scottish town where he has been dispatched to purchase land for his oil company has caused him to take a fresh look at his life as a Houston based executive. He has come to appreciate the value of nature, the value of tradition, and more important, the value of love. Mac has witnessed the sensuous relationship between Gordon, the town barkeep and accountant, and Stella, the owner of the town's hotel. He has, perhaps for the first time, realized that love can be a natural and an uncomplicated phenomenon. He envies Gordon so much that he is convinced that he has fallen in love with Stella.

Under the influence of a wee bit of 40 year old Scotch whiskey Mac suggests that Gordon and he swap places, that Gordon take his job in Houston and that he move into Gordon's position. Of course, Stella would be part of the deal, remaining in Scotland, now with Mac instead of Gordon. At least that is Mac's fantasy.

When Mac does return to his upscale apartment in Houston he gazes out on the city lights, listens to the city noises and reflects on the contrast between these sights and sounds and the pastoral ideal of the Scottish coastal village. He places photos of the village and its inhabitants on his bulletin board. He empties his coat pockets of the sand the shells that he has collected.

The scene shifts to the one phone booth in the Scottish village. The phone rings. Is it Mac? Is he trying to reattach himself to a culture that seems to be so strange and so beautiful, a culture that in a few days changed Mac's perception of the possibilities for happiness. Is it Mac trying to connect himself to Stella? Is it Mac trying to cope with a conflict between himself and the system of land acquisition and oil profits that made him numb to his own humanity? Is it Mac taking a step toward exit? The phone in the red booth in the small Scottish town continues to ring, unanswered.

Fade to black.

The End.

Chapter Twelve

Conclusion

One important notion that is suggested by the Legend is the distinction between our private and our public persona. All of the people in these stories are confronted with the problem of dual roles and the reality of conflict between these roles. There was, I suppose, a time when the private role of people dominated their lives without them having to think much about it. When we produced for ourselves what we needed, we did not have to become part of an organized or social system. When we could protect ourselves and provide for necessary services, we could do so without sharing these aspects of our labor with others. But a dominant, perhaps the dominant, reality of modern life is a division of labor among elements of a larger (public) society. The benefits of this aspect of modernity are legion. The costs are not clearly understood. The specific danger revealed by the Legend is that our private selves can become lost in our public selves, that our individuality can drown in the currents of the organizational sea, that we can lose what we are and become what we do.

The solution to this problem, for most of us, cannot be to get rid of the public role. Most of us would wither on the vine without the nurturing of the benefits of our modern existence. Most of us would make unhappy hermits. The

Legend does suggest, however, that the viability of the individual self (we might even say soul) is a prerequisite to the usefulness of the individual as a unit of a social system. Before any of the characters in these stories could be of any meaningful use to any organized system, they had to be of use to themselves. Some of the heroes of these stories are able to meld the function of an organization with the functioning of themselves. Some of the heroes chose other paths.

We accept the idea that the happy synthesis of person and system is a functions of the leader. We assign to the leader the responsibility to prevent the alienation of the individual. Yet the push of person toward system values, or the pull of the person away from these, the Legend tells us, can and should be the responsibility of followers.

Another lesson of the Legend is that living successful organizational lives is an iterative process. There are no buttons to push, no computer programs to use, that will generate a condition of happiness. Organizational life is not static. Our individual needs are dynamic. As we progress through the macro stages of life, and the micro day to day adjustments as well, our needs change. Our internal conflicts and stresses also change. What worked for the characters in the stories at one point in time, failed to work at another time. The Legend tells us that we cannot navigate through our years of organizational life without constant attention to the rudder.

The final lesson of the Legend is the requirement for self-reliance. The stories illustrate the seductive nature of modern organizations. The organized system is designed to deliver valued goods and services to us as clients, customers, or constituents. The fact that the modern organization came into existence in the bureaucratic form and continues to flourish in this form is evidence that the mission aspect of organizational purpose can be and often is well served. The trap for the individual member of a modern organization is the implication that the organization necessarily serves its members, as well as its public. The Legend makes it clear that organizations, by their very nature, are not nurturers of their members. This is not to say that organizations cannot or do not nurture their members. This is to say that the nurturing of members is not a predictable outcome. If we assign the task of the nurturing of our individuality, of the nurturing our souls, to the organization, we are taking a great risk. The generic solution is neither to withdraw participation nor to adopt a cynical and distrustful posture. The solution is to take responsibility for the fulfillment of our own purpose , in the words of Voltaire's Candide, to "cultivate our own garden." (Voltaire 1990)

References

Argyris, Chris, *Personality and Organization*, New York:Harper, 1957.

Aristotle, *Nicomachean Ethics*, New York:Macmillan, 1962.

Barnard, Chester I.,*The Functions of the Executive*,Cambridge:Harvard University Press, 1938.

Chaleff, Ira, *The Courageous Follower*, San Francisco: Berett-Koehler, 1998.

Dickens, Charles, A Christmas Carol, London: King Penguin Books, 1984.

Dreyfus, Hubert L. and Dreyfus, Stuart E., *Mind Over Machines: The Power of Human Expertise in the Era of the Computer*, New York: Free Press,1986.

Etzioni, Amitai, *Modern Organizations*, New Jersey:Prentice-Hall, 1964.

Goodsell, C and Murray, N., ed. *Public Administration Illuminated and Inspired by the Arts*, New York: Praeger, 1995.

Hobbes, Thomas, *Leviathan*, New York:Viking Press, 1982.

Michels, Robert, *Political Parties*, Glencoe: Free Press, 1949.

Maslow, Abraham, *Motivation and Personality*, New York:Harper,1954.

References

Michels, Robert, *Political Parties*, Glencoe: Free Press, 1949.

Morgan, Gareth, *Imagin.i.zation; New Mindsets for Seeing, Organizing, and Managing*, San Francisco: Berrett-Koehler, 1997.

Persig, Robert, *Zen and the Art of Motorcycle Maintenance*, New York: William Morrow, 1974.

Roethlisberger, F.J., *Management and Morale*, Cambridge: Harvard University Press, 1941.

Voltaire, Francois-Marie, *Candide*, New York: Penguin (1990)

Waldo, D., *The Novelist on Organization and Administration: An inquiry into the relationship between two worlds*, Berkeley: Institute of Governmental Studies, 1968.

Weber, Max, *Essays in Sociology*, edited by H.H. Gerth and C. Wright Mills, Oxford: Oxford University Press, 1946.

Weick, Karl E., "Technology as Equivoque: Sensemaking in New Technologies" in Technology and Organizations, edited by P.S. Goodman et.al., Jossey-Bass: San Francisco, 1990.

Weick, K.E., and Roberts, K.H., "Collective Mind and Organizational Reliability: The case of flight operations on an aircraft carrier deck." Administrative Science Quarterly, 38, 357-381, 1993.

White, David, *The Heart Aroused*, New York: Doubleday, 1996.

Index

A Few Good Men, 91,99,103
alienation, 118,126,128-130, 134
Apollo 13, 18,19,96
Argyris, Chris, 20
Aristotle, 3,6,11,109,116
Barnard, Chester I., 14,20,21,119,120
bureaucracy, 15-20,38,72,74,77,108,113
Catch 22, 71,80
Chaleff, Ira, 124
Challenger, 18,19
chaos, 17,37,38,108
conformity, 118,120,124,126
coping, 118-120,124,126,128,130
creative rebellion, 126
Dickens, Charles, 59,60,63,66,67
Dirty Harry, 98
Dreyfus and Dreyfus, 18
Electric Horseman, 49,50,92,112,130
Etzioni, Amitai, 13
Executive Suite, 83-86,89,91
exit, 130-132
Federalist Papers, 81
formal organization, 24
future, 105-109,113
Goodsell, C and Murray, N, 9
Groundhog Day, 60-69
happiness,3,7,11,21,23,45,52,59,65,69,83,96,102,
106,108,109,114,116,130,132
harmony, 12,17,21,23,27,51,53,73,92,93,115,126,127
hierarchy, 6,18,24,41,72,74,75,76,81,82,87
holograph, 14,15
Hawthorne Studies, 20
High Noon,13,98,131
Hobbes, Thomas,37
Human Relations, 20
informal organization, 24
In Pursuit of Honor, 49,52, 57

Index

Iron Law of Oligarchy, 81
isolation, 64,93leader, 6,7,11,13,20,21,47,74 -78,120,134
Local Hero, 11,14,126,134
Lost in America, 5,49,54 -56,113,124
Madison, James, 81
marty, 130,131
Maslow, Abraham, 6,117
Michels, Robert,81
Morgan,Gareth, 13,15,16,37
Network, 4,12,23,24,29,37,38,79,108,109,128,129
1984, 14,105,106,109
Patton, 71,79
Persig, Robert, 1
personal transformation,124
Peter Principle,78
professionalism, 25,27,91
purpose, 5,8,25,38,39,42 - 46,49,70,78,84,89,116,134
rational, 9,16,21,43,44,59,80,98
rite of passage, 120-124
Roberts, K.H, 17
Roethlisberger, F.J., 20
role, 50,51,54,57,68,89,92,96,133
role conflict, 57,58,67,92
Rollerball, 105,109-113
Silkwood, 13,15,130
socialization, 12-14,89,120
specialization, 71-74,83,84,92
The Caine Mutiny, 7,22,71,75,76,108,121
The Fountainhead, 99
The Right Stuff, 91-97
Twelve O'clock High, 4,7,12,19,21,37,39-47,71,72,92,118-120,124-128,130
2001 A Space Odyssey, 19,105-108
uncooperative rebel, 128,129
Voltaire, Francois-Marie, 135
Waldo, D., 7,8
Weber, Max, 15,37,38
Weick, Karl E., 17,18
zone of indifference, 14,15,20,120